C000090018

THE EFFECTIVE LEADER

The Effective Leader

JAMES DUNN

KINGSWAY PUBLICATIONS
EASTBOURNE

Copyright © James Dunn 1995

The right of James Dunn to be identified
as author of this work has been asserted by him in
accordance with the Copyright, Designs
and Patents Act 1988.

First published 1995

All rights reserved.
No part of this publication may be reproduced or
transmitted in any form or by any means, electronic
or mechanical, including photocopy, recording, or any
information storage and retrieval system, without
permission in writing from the publisher.

Unless otherwise indicated, biblical quotations are from the
New International Version © 1973, 1978, 1984 by the
International Bible Society. Use is also made of the
Living Bible (TLB) © Tyndale House Publishers 1971;
the Authorised Version (AV), Crown copyright; and
The New Testament in Modern English © J.B. Phillips,
1960, 1972 (PHILLIPS).

ISBN 0 85476 354 6

Produced by Bookprint Creative Services
P.O. Box 827, BN21 3YJ, England, for
KINGSWAY PUBLICATIONS LTD
Lottbridge Drove, Eastbourne, E Sussex BN23 6NT.
Printed in Great Britain.

Contents

Foreword

The Duke in *Twelfth Night* at one stage writes a letter with the words:

> But be not afraid of greatness: some men are born great, some achieve greatness, and some have greatness thrust upon them.

The same could be said of leadership: 'Be not afraid of leadership: some men (and these days women) are born to lead, some achieve leadership, and some have leadership thrust upon them.' Whichever category, or gender, you happen to be in, this book is for you!

This is a book which looks at the issues of leadership as well as the principles of leadership, at the theology as well as the practice, and at the wide view across the whole stage as well as the detailed performance by an individual in a quiet moment.

It is unashamedly Christian, and is relevant whatever a leader's denomination. It is also relevant for whatever level of leadership a person may be at—the very top or some intermediate stage. While primarily set in the context of the local church, its matter is equally acceptable for those serving in Christian organisations or in other spheres.

Some might criticise its lack of depth. But that is one of its strengths. This book covers the whole gamut of leadership, and does so succinctly, putting the strands into an overall perspective.

It enables the reader to identify his or her strengths and weaknesses and thus to go away to build on those strengths and to focus on overcoming the weaknesses. This book will make an ideal manual for anyone wishing to run courses on the subject of leadership.

Several years ago I read John Haggai's book *Lead On*, and was struck by the fact that, of his twelve chapters on different facets of leadership, he devoted a whole chapter to the cruciality of energy: 'Nothing important was ever achieved by someone with no energy.' Did James Dunn include this topic, I wondered before I began? The answer is yes, for it is one of the nine key characteristics identified in Chapter Two.

Of the book's four sections—the challenge, the style, the vision, and the strategies—the third is broken down into four component parts and is critical for the understanding of the rest. It is not just that 'where there is no vision the people perish', but where there is no vision the church perishes, and where there is no vision the leader perishes. Vision is both corporate and personal. Of the many tests in the book, that in Chapter Seven will enable you to assess how good is your vision just now. Others have written more fully on how to find your vision, and there are more ways than those suggested here. But making a start is essential, and this is a book full of such starters.

I therefore personally commend it very warmly indeed. James Dunn has done the Christian community a welcome service by writing this book, which comes with perception, example and challenge. If you are not prepared to change, or don't see the need for change, don't read *The Effective Leader*! In Tom Houston's book *King David* four paths to successful leadership are outlined. One is the need to continually develop. King David did not write all his psalms one Tuesday evening—they came from a lifetime of experience and trauma and trust in God. Likewise if we are to be successful we must continually be willing to learn from others, and grow accordingly. I trust through the reading of this book you will allow yourself to grow. It is one of the marks of a true leader.

Peter Brierley

Introduction

Have you ever wondered what gives groups and organisations, even whole societies, their unique and varied identities and makes them 'tick over' in the ways that they do? One answer is people!

Some years ago I attended a seminar organised by a major company for its UK management. The opening address to delegates was given by a senior figure from within the company. He began with a wry comment about organisations. 'Most of them,' he said, 'contain three sorts of people: those who make things happen, those who watch things happen and those who don't know what's happening!'

Sometimes I feel that the same can be said of the church at large. (Incidentally, any who are curious to discover the category in which they belong should be warned. The process of finding out can sometimes lead to a damaged ego!)

This book is for those who believe themselves to be at the 'cutting edge'; who sense that their role is to effect change and 'make things happen'. Primarily it is for Christians, lay people as well as clergy, whose job or vocation requires them to exert some kind of leadership influence within their church, or perhaps an organisation associated with it.

The material it contains does not represent a theology of leadership. Much has been written about this already and is in print elsewhere. Nor is this a textbook of management theory for Christians of the 'safe to read' sort. Rather it is a workbook, designed as a resource to help those involved or about to become involved in Christian leadership to obtain a practical grasp of the key competencies required.

The contemporary Christian scene is dynamic; opportunities for expansion and accomplishment are everywhere.

Do you think the work of harvesting will not begin until the summer ends four months from now? [challenges the eager, perceptive Christ] **Look around you! Vast fields of human souls are ripening all around us, and are ready now for reaping (Jn 4: 35, TLB).**

The overwhelming need is for leaders; those who can orchestrate the activities of others, harnessing their skills and talents. Leaders who know what to do and who have the capacity and energy to take things forward.

As the sense of the importance of leadership grows, so does the myth that it is a mystical quality possessed by a few charismatic individuals. This book shows, in detail, that leadership can be learned—that it encompasses a set of processes and a style of behaviour that can be consciously nurtured.

Clearly, Christian leadership is not just about exercising certain skills in professional ways. But, without detracting from the essentially spiritual nature of any Christian undertaking, the fact remains that many of the problems facing churches and voluntary Christian organisations today are management problems. Arguably, a major cause of hindered progress is poor management; of people and resources, of projects and communications, and of relationships.

Given the pressures and complexities of twentieth-century living and the rapid pace of change, it is foolish not to acknowledge the need for professional as well as spiritual competencies among Christian leaders.

The old adage 'Leaders are born, not made' is only part truth. It is necessary to possess certain basic qualities and aptitudes, but these have to be developed before they can be of any use. Leaders have to be made as well as born.

Also important is the context or 'environment' in which leadership occurs, and here the church situation is perhaps unique. It has to be said that the challenges and problems, even frustrations, facing those who have to exercise leadership within, say, the framework of a local church or a diocese are likely to be quite different from those normally encountered in a strictly business setting.

This is partly due to the voluntary and often transient nature of the teams or groups of people with whom they have to work. A bishop lacks direct authority to deploy his manpower exactly as and when he likes. A pastor may have to operate with a 'management' team over which he does not have complete control and which can change, suddenly, before it has time to settle. House-group leaders, themselves volunteers, often face the problem of having to persuade others to go along with their ideas first, in order to get anything done. All this serves to underscore the importance of context, and the need to bear it in mind when developing an effective leadership strategy.

It is perfectly possible for leadership skills to develop through experience alone; by watching what others do, then by 'having a go' and seeing what happens—a kind of trial-and-error approach. Sometimes this is the only way to learn. However, it can also be a very slow way.

This book will help you think closely about the skills and attitudes which Christian leaders need, and will guide you towards finding practical ways of acquiring and applying them in your own situation.

Part One—Accepting the Challenge introduces the subject, and outlines the kinds of things that face the person who would be a Christian leader, eg, the nature of leadership and what, in particular, makes Christian leadership 'Christian'; the need for leaders and the calibre of person required and, finally, the task: what exactly is it that leaders have to do?

Part Two—Developing an Effective Style explains how the leadership process works. It explores the uses of power, the parts people play and the significance of the context or environment in which it all takes place. There are ways suggested by which you can identify and develop a leadership style which suits the situation you may find yourself in when operating as a leader.

Part Three—Leading With Vision covers in detail the essentials of leadership strategy. It directs attention to the major issues which all leaders have to address, eg, creating and communicating vision; implementing change; developing and using the talent of others and showing how practical agendas for action may be devised in each case.

Part Four—Successful Leadership Strategies provides a basis for reviewing the main messages of the book. It creates a focus by leading you to consider several key questions like: Is my leadership style appropriate? Am I communicating my vision effectively? It will help you to establish your own action plan for bringing about specific improvements in areas where you have identified a need.

In Parts One, Two and Three, at the end of each chapter, there is a 'Key Points Summary' and a 'Guide for Action', both of which allow you to reflect on what you have read and to think about the actions you may need to take before moving to the next section.

You will need a Bible, paper and pen(cil), and a willingness to work. The rest should follow.

PART ONE

Accepting the Challenge

I have to admit I was apprehensive, Lord, that day you took us up into the hills. We knew why we were going. It was clear in your manner. You were going to choose—to choose the ones you wanted to work with you.

Of course, I knew I wouldn't be chosen. I had no special talents. Just an ordinary guy who works with his hands.

So I wasn't surprised when you singled out the wealthy businessman. You'd need financial backing for what you had in mind. Nor when you chose the writer. Your speeches would need scripting. You'd need people who could put ideas across, who could draft your manifesto. No surprise either when you chose the multilinguist. If you had your eyes on a worldwide venture there'd be plenty of translation work to be done. Then there was the public relations overseer, the chap to handle the media, and, quite properly, a couple of specialists on religious matters.

And so it went on. Every one a wise choice, your decisions quite rational: people essential to the team you needed. And then you'd finished. The rest of us watched, a little embarrassed. Yes, I admit it; rejection hurt us just a little. But none of us was surprised. Clearly, you'd made the right choices.

Then you turned to the twelve of us and smiled. Imagine our surprise. 'Come on,' you said, 'there's a job to be done.'

Chapter One

THE LEADERSHIP FACTOR

Individual leaders, not organisations, create excellence.
Anonymous

In those days Israel had no King; everyone did as they saw fit
(Judg 21:25).

Why are leaders needed?

Picture an army about to enter a battle, or a company employing people to make a product, or a church trying to fulfil its mission within a community. Clearly, many factors will be at work, shaping events, influencing outcomes. But in each case there is one factor which has to be present and whose influence must predominate if the enterprise is to succeed. This is the much talked about, often misunderstood phenomenon known as 'leadership'.

As a topic, leadership has a rather dated air about it. To some, it smacks of trench warfare and imperial administration. It implies setting one man up above another and raises spectres of élites and privileged classes. 'Why is leadership necessary?' they ask. 'Surely a group of intelligent, well-meaning individuals can tackle any situation facing them without the need for one to be the leader?' Indeed there is sometimes a tendency to play down the importance of individuals as leaders and to favour instead better organisation structures and systems as the key to effectiveness.

But the fact remains: any activity which binds people in the service of a common task, whether it be winning a war, running a company or 'being the church', needs that special input which comes from certain individuals and which is called, for want of a better word, leadership. Without it there can be no real progress towards any objective.

In the days of Shamgar son of Anath, in the days of Jael, the roads were abandoned; travellers took to winding paths. Village life in Israel ceased, ceased until I, Deborah, arose, arose a mother in Israel (Judg 5:6-7).

Anyone who has been responsible for organising or co-ordinating the efforts of others in order to get things done, knows this. Surveys which try to assess things like morale, growth and effectiveness within organisations usually reveal the significance of the leadership role. Where statistics are gathered, they tend to show that the calibre and ability of those running the organisation, or even just parts of it, are crucial. Churches, house groups, Saturday clubs and special 'one-off' events are all dependent on those who organise and lead them.

Organisations whose business or professional performance keeps improving, and who move steadily in the direction of their chosen goals, show the workings of energetic leadership. Churches and fellowships that forge ahead, gaining ground, growing in numbers and spiritual maturity and who make an impact on their community, give evidence of the same principle at work. These things do not happen on their own. Usually they are the products of effective leadership.

The converse is also true. Organisations and groups that lack leadership often find themselves and their work going into decline, and leaders who cannot or do not lead may have to acknowledge that their non-effectiveness is contributing to the downward slide.

Those in positions of leadership should face the fact that they represent the 'cutting edge' at all times and that the responsibility for achieving results rests mainly with them.

These are potent claims which in turn give rise to questions about the nature of the task itself. What of the view that it requires an innate capability possessed by only a few? What part, if any, do technique and behavioural style play?

In a word, 'What is leadership, and what does it take to be a leader?' Is there some trick to it; something that if we could learn it it would transform us? Are there models we should imitate—great men we can learn from?

What is leadership?

Secular literature on the subject abounds with definitions. Some are helpful; others less so, to the point of being slightly misleading. There is a tendency to over-emphasise the idea of control, focusing on the ability to influence and even manipulate the actions of others.

Some Christian views of leadership, reflected by what is said and written, show a tendency to veer in the opposite direction, stressing the importance of the individual and the need to allow him or her to develop and realise their full potential.

In 1970 Vic Feather, then General Secretary of the British Trades Union Congress, said: 'What industry needs is not bosses but leaders.' He was distinguishing between two quite separate approaches to the job of working with others in order to get things done.

The first is based on the assumption that people need to be driven if anything is to be achieved. By insisting that 'bossing' tactics were short-sighted and inappropriate, Feather condemned this ruthless, task-orientated approach. Bossing people around may get them to comply with a course of action, but it will not necessarily gain their commitment to it, and it is the latter which is more likely be needed in the long run.

The alternative to driving people is to lead them. That this approach can and does succeed, and that it is preferable, is based on the assumption that people want to achieve, are capable of acting in an adult way and are keen to accept responsibility.

However, the leadership issue remains complex and it is too simplistic to think of it as being merely a matter of adopting a people-centred approach compared to one which is task-centred. Rather, it is a special kind of influence which works in situations where results are needed. It touches people and involves them in the process. Often these 'results' do not exactly coincide with personal goals, but they require a spirit of togetherness and a co-ordination of effort if they are to be achieved. This means that as well as a blossoming forth of individuals, there often has to be a bending of wills and sometimes of backs in the interests of reaching a common goal.

True leadership creates and sustains these conditions.

Leaders and managers—are they different?

The concept of leadership is sometimes better understood by attempting to contrast it with that of management.

Clearly the words 'leader' and 'manager' are not inter-changeable terms. In fact they represent two quite separate concepts, although there are similarities between them. There are also some important differences which must be observed. Abraham Zaleznik, in a much-praised *Harvard Business Review* article, 'Managers and Leaders: are they different?', argued that mere managers tend to adopt impersonal, passive attitudes towards getting the job done; they solve problems along the way by effecting compromises among people and ideas; they see themselves as conservators and regulators of an existing order; they worry more about people's roles than the people themselves; they perpetuate existing processes, generate bureaucratic red tape and display little directness and warmth.

By contrast, leaders adopt a personal and active attitude towards goals. They develop a compelling vision of the organisation's future, and translate that vision into reality by constantly articulating it and by concentrating on the keys to its success. They motivate others to embrace it and remain deeply involved at the heart of things, spurring the actions needed to carry it out.

At the risk of making it sound too trite: 'Managers do things right; leaders do the right things.'

The reality is that leadership calls for a bit of both. Understanding these distinctions will help you to appreciate more fully the challenge you face as a leader.

The word 'lead' comes from a common European root word meaning 'a path, road or the course of a ship at sea'. Putting it bluntly, churches, organisations and companies, Christian or not, that have decided, for whatever reason, that they are not going anywhere, should forget about leadership and settle for management.

What makes Christian leadership 'Christian'?

I referred earlier to the context or cultural setting in which the leader operates. However, it is naïve to suppose that leadership which takes place within a so-called 'Christian' context is, by definition, Christian. In fact it may be no different from the kind which is exercised elsewhere. Circumstances and cultural norms can complicate or simplify the task without determining its essential nature.

Is there such a thing as Christian leadership? Might it be more appropriate to describe it as leadership which is exercised by Christians? At the risk of sounding equivocal, the answer to both questions is 'yes'.

There is a leadership influence which takes character from the fact that those exercising it are Christians. There is also a unique method of leadership which may fairly be described as Christian.

Christian leadership, by definition, must have something to do with Christ, and therein lies the first clue as to what it is. Colossians 1:18 is one of several scriptures which declare that Christ 'is the head of the body, the church'.

This relationship between head and body works both ways. The head receives input from the body—joy, pain, strain and so on. At the same time, the head controls the activity of the body, making decisions and implementing them by initiating and co-ordinating the actions of its members.

Here is a short 'True or False' quiz. Completing it will sharpen your thinking on the topic.

Christian Leadership   **TRUE / FALSE?**

1. Human leadership is not necessary in the Christian church.
2. Christian leaders take the place of Christ, for all practical purposes.
3. Christian leaders represent Christ, but don't replace him.
4. Christ is not actively leading the church today. He has left that to the earthly leaders he has appointed.
5. The Christian leader's task is to get others to follow Christ.
6. The Christian leader's role is purely administrative, to ensure that 'all things are done decently and in order'.
7. The Christian leader is a channel through whom Christ functions as a leader.
8. The Christian leader is only a 'mouthpiece', reminding people of what the Bible says.

Here are a few comments with which to compare your own thoughts:

1. This has to be False. The New Testament is studded with examples of people exercising leadership, quite legitimately it seems, within the Christian church. The often-quoted words 'God's methods are men' hold good.
2. False. Christian leaders don't have that kind of autonomy! Problems have been caused within churches by leaders who have tried to take the place of Christ, acting as though they were the head, and sustaining a relationship with the

members which rightly belongs to him.

3. True. But this is a statement which raises other questions, eg, 'Represent Christ in what way and to what extent?'

4. False. This is a bit like the second statement. Divine appointment does not equal full autonomy; nor does it carry authority to act in any name other than that of Christ.

5. True. But that's not all there is to it.

6. False. The New Testament uses several words to describe the Christian leader; 'administrator' or 'manager' is only one of them.

7. Nice one! This is True, but it leaves open the question as to how this occurs.

8. False. This statement, like some of the earlier ones, expresses a limited view of what Christian leadership is about.

There are three key areas where the difference between Christian leadership and that of other kinds can be noted. These are:

- Models
- Motives
- Morals and values

Models

Numerous words are used in the New Testament to describe the Christian leader: 'shepherd', one who cares and guards; 'steward', one who acts responsibly in relation to his master's property; 'overseer', someone who watches over a situation and is ready to act where necessary to maintain order; 'administrator', a manager and organiser of resources.

These focus attention on the leader's actions and can clearly apply to any leader in any leadership situation. There is, however, a word found in the New Testament which depicts an attitude or stance from which actions flow; it is never used of leaders in the Christian setting. The word is *archon* and it means 'to rule over' or 'dominate'.

Words spoken by Jesus, recorded in Matthew 20:25–27, acknowledge this kind of leadership but disown the principle on which it is based:

> **You know that the rulers of the Gentiles lord it over them, and their high officials exercise authority over them. Not so with you. Instead, whoever wants to become great among you must be your servant, and whoever wants to be first must be your slave.**

The design of it and the actions it spawns are declared foreign to the kingdom of God and to those who belong in it.

These words also warn against adopting the leadership models of the outside world. There are really only two kingdoms in operation: the kingdom of God and the kingdoms of this world— which are in the charge of Satan.

> **The devil led him up to a high place and showed him in an instant all the kingdoms of the world. And he said to him, 'I will give you all their authority and splendour, for it has been given to me, and I can give it to anyone I want to' (Lk 4:5).**

Arguably, then, all systems of leadership ultimately trace their origins and associations back to one or the other.

Leadership by domination, with its accompanying need to drive and control and force, features the way in which the kingdoms of this world operate. The kind of leadership Christ advocates is completely different and is modelled squarely on the concept of servanthood. This is plain from these words—and from Christ's personal testimony and example:

> **I am among you as one who serves (Lk 22:27).**

The words of Peter the apostle, recorded later, confirm this view:

> **Be shepherds of God's flock that is under your care, serving as overseers. . .not lording it over those entrusted**

to you, but being examples (1 Pet 5:2–3).

What a contrast between this and the success-orientated, career-minded, power-hungry spirit all too prevalent among the leaders and influence brokers of present-day society.

While the actions of a servant are important and worth noting, it is the servant attitude which is more significant. Action is influenced by attitude, and this includes the way in which the personality is projected. It is in this context that the cryptic words of John the Baptist are best understood:

He must become greater; I must become less (Jn 3:30).

However, it is wise to keep this concept of servanthood in perspective; it does not imply servility. There are more references in the New Testament to the Christian leader as a servant of God than as a servant of people. This shows where the priority of his actions ought to lie as well as his character, and safeguards his leadership from subjugation to the democratic wish or from manipulation by one or two smart operators. This is aptly summed up in words written by Paul the apostle to the church at Corinth:

We make it our goal to please him (2 Cor 5:9).

Effective leadership provides a catalyst for action, and the Christian leader, adopting the stance of servant, focuses the attention of those he leads on the purpose and plan of God as it affects them, and facilitates the actions needed to bring it about.

Motives

Motives are the forces at work within us driving and to a degree controlling our actions. This inner drive, or 'motivation', should be discerned from 'movement' which may be the result of external pressure. Sometimes a jolt is needed, but leaders have to be careful lest they yield to undue pressure.

The counsel given by the Apostle Paul is of particular

importance to Christian leaders:

Do not let the world around you squeeze you into its mould (Rom 12:2, J. B. PHILLIPS).

Motives are significant. As well as prompting action, they often provide the clues which explain action. Probably the ultimate question asked of every human being concerning his life and action will be:'Why?'

There is a tendency to concentrate on 'what' and 'how' and 'when' and 'where', but 'why' is the most important question: Why do we do what we do? Why do we want to lead?

The reasons why people are attracted into leadership roles vary considerably, but among the more common are: a sense of power; money; opportunities to influence people and events; the need to control what is happening; a desire for recognition; pride; egotism. These concerns are mostly self-centred and reflect what individuals feel they are most likely to get from being in a leadership position.

An important distinguishing motive of Christian leadership is:

Selflessness

The time-honoured words of Peter, great apostle and leader of men, ring with particular emphasis:

... serving as overseers—not because you must, but because you are willing, as God wants you to be; not greedy for money but eager to serve; not lording it over those entrusted to you, but being examples to the flock (1 Pet 5:2–3).

Aspiring to leadership in this context is a worthy ambition, but it isn't something to be pursued from selfish motives. Christian leadership, founded on the concept of servanthood, is primarily for others: God first, people next.

Another driving force which distinguishes Christian leadership from its secular counterparts is:

A sense of vocation

Some situations cry out for leadership, and history affords many instances of those who, in response to the need of their times, rose up and began to lead. Witness the actions of Oliver Cromwell during the English Civil War or Winston Churchill during the Second World War.

There is, however, a call to leadership which carries more weight and has more significance than the voice of circumstance. The Christian leader is someone who has heard from God. Moses heard in the empty wilderness as he stood before a burning bush. Paul the apostle heard as he travelled the road to Damascus.

There are not many who can claim that their call to leadership came in such spectacular circumstances, but true Christian leadership is carried by a conviction which amounts to a sense of God's appointment to the task. This kind of leadership is a privilege; the opportunity and the potential to lead are God-given and should be received and cherished as a gift.

Obedience

This is epitomised in the words of the apostles Peter and John, spoken at a time when the direction of their leadership was being challenged:

Judge for yourselves whether it is right in God's sight to obey you rather than God (Acts 4:19).

The same motive spurred Nehemiah to continue his building project when a proposal was put to him that he stop and take part in a discussion about strategy. He saw this for what it was—a diversion—and his response, sent by messenger, read like this:

I am carrying on a great project and cannot go down. Why should the work stop while I leave it and go down to you? (Neh 6:3).

This kind of obedience goes beyond merely the determination to stay true to yourself and to stand by your own convictions.

Joshua, who succeeded Moses as the leader of the peoples of Israel, was counselled at the start of his career to make obedience one of the motives of his leadership:

Be careful to obey all the law my servant Moses gave you; do not turn from it to the right or to the left, that you may be successful wherever you go. Do not let this Book of the Law depart from your mouth; meditate on it day and night, so that you may be careful to do everything written in it (Josh 1: 7–8).

His obedience was to be based on his knowledge of the word of God and the will of God, passed on to him by Moses. This contained details which would fashion the character and pattern of daily living and also of the unique life plan to be followed if the people, including himself, were to discover their special destiny.

Joshua's leadership of his people was to reflect, among other things, unswerving obedience to God's way. His responsibility was twofold: to make sure he understood the directions, and to have the courage and strength of character to put them into effect through his leadership. All serious Christian leadership is motivated by obedience of this sort.

Sensitivity

Though sometimes regarded as a quality which nice people have, when seen in relation to leadership it is clearly a motivating factor which influences its nature and outcomes.

Christian leadership works by sensitivity. It is possible to be so wrapped up in ourselves and in our own sense of what is right and wrong, good or bad—self-absorption is the jargon phrase—that we become insensitive to what might be going on around us.

Insensitivity is unhealthy. It comes from:

- Assuming you know the expectations and needs of others without discussing them.
- Treating everyone the same, regardless of their differences.
- Viewing people as machines; tools for getting things done.

- Seeing people as they once were, not recognising changes or improvements in them.
- Believing everyone should respond the way *you* would in the same situation.

Sensitivity is the art of getting inside another person. The stark words of Ezekiel the prophet are a graphic illustration of what it means:

> **I came to the exiles ... And there, where they were living, I sat among them for seven days—overwhelmed (Ezek 3:15).**

Of course sensitive leadership does not stop at this—it acts to fulfil the needs and expectations it finds there—but it does take the trouble to find out what those needs are.

Love

This is probably the most powerful motive there is; it results in leadership of a special kind. Jesus described the difference between leadership that works by love and that which is propelled by other considerations:

> **The good shepherd lays down his life for the sheep. The hired hand is not the shepherd who owns the sheep. So when he sees the wolf coming, he abandons the sheep and runs away ... because he is a hired hand and cares nothing for the sheep (Jn 10:11–13).**

For 'love' we might here read 'sacrifice'; it is 'what you are prepared to give up for it'. When leadership is allied to love, it assumes its most potent form. Napoleon Bonaparte, one of the world's greatest leaders, while pacing the shores of his lonely island prison, turned to his companions and uttered these memorable words: 'Alexander, Charlemagne and myself founded empires. But on what did we found them? On force. Jesus Christ founded his on love and today there are millions who would die for him.'

Paul the apostle, writer, traveller, pioneer missionary, builder of churches and leader *par excellence*, declared the secret of his motivation:

If we are out of our mind, it is for the sake of God; if we are in our right mind, it is for you. For Christ's love compels us (2 Cor 5:13–14).

The towering sentiments of 1 Corinthians 13, penned in praise of love, support the view that as a driving force it has no equal.

Christian leadership is a leadership of love.

Morals and values

Most people have a personal philosophy—a code, a design for living and a definite, albeit in some cases ill-defined, pattern of things worth while. If you do not think this is true, then ask this question of yourself: 'What are the three things so important to me that without them life would not be worth living?'

Initially, you may begin by listing lots of things, changing and transposing as you go along, becoming more deliberate, reflective and then quite philosophical about your final list.

Morals and values guide us towards seeing what things give meaning and worth to our life. They govern behaviour. This is especially true where leadership is concerned. The leader's morals and values will tend to be reflected by the way in which the leadership task is carried out. Some leaders are uncertain of themselves in these areas. Few possess a well-articulated system. Yet most of the things we do are directed by basic attitudes towards ourselves and others, by our ideas of success and by our concepts of personal responsibility.

Morals operate as a kind of internal yardstick, determining the essential nature of a decision or action.

Values are difficult to identify objectively. They may change with time and circumstance; often they cannot be precisely calculated. However, they remain measures of the worth we give to things in our lives, enabling us to sift the important from the unimportant.

It is in this area of morals and values that Christian leadership acquires a further distinctiveness. There are principles which determine behaviour and relationships; priorities which set the agenda for action. Many are outlined in words that Paul the apostle wrote to Timothy, an aspiring New Testament leader:

Now the overseer must be... Deacons, likewise, are to be... (1 Tim 3:2–12).

One word encompasses much of what is required: integrity. Integrity means unity of life and consistency of action.

The Christian leader has to get his moral and spiritual act together. Whether integrity of life or of purpose, it matters not. Moral lopsidedness or inappropriate value judgements on the leader's part will impair the Christian leadership process. But it will be enhanced when in the hands of Christians who score highly in the moral and personal maturity stakes; who establish and maintain reputations for fair, equitable dealing, for friendliness, for hospitality and whose social and domestic relationships are sound.

The worth and effectiveness of Christian leadership are influenced by the integrity of those who lead.

From the foregoing it may be seen that even though the leader is a Christian, it does not follow that he or she will lead in a Christian way. The essence of Christian leadership is found in the *model*, the *motives* and the *morals and values* by which it operates.

The challenge of Christian leadership lies in understanding and accepting these as the norm.

KEY POINTS SUMMARY

The key purpose of this chapter is to focus attention on the fact of leadership, highlighting the need for it, the nature of it and the unique features of Christian leadership.

Leadership provides a catalyst for action; it is a special kind of influence which works in situations where results are needed.

The concepts of management and leadership are intertwined, but there are important differences between them which have to be understood.

Christian leadership has several distinguishing features:

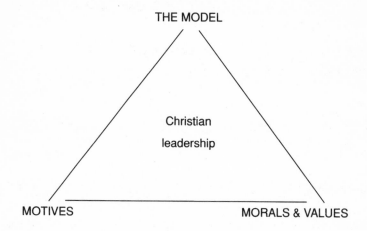

GUIDE FOR ACTION

- List three tasks or situations in which you are expected to give leadership.
- Conduct an honest self-appraisal: discern your motives, morals and values.
- Develop an individual system of personal priorities.
- Create time to think and meditate. Consider what you will give up in order to do this.
- Do things that promote the continuing development of your inner, spiritual resources.
- Develop a creative approach to experience; learn to 'fail constructively'.

Part Four of this book, 'Successful Leadership Strategies', offers some helpful guidelines.

Chapter Two

THE LEADERSHIP PERSONALITY

The best test of whether one is a qualified leader is to find out whether anyone is following.

D. E. Hoste

Select seven men, wise and full of the Holy Spirit, who are well thought of by everyone; and we will put them in charge. . . (Acts 6:3, TLB).

Leadership gives cohesion and purpose to the actions of people when they are working together. But it is fascinating to watch what happens during the early stages when someone new starts bringing their influence to bear upon a group. Careful observers have noted that often the first thing any would-be leader has to do is prove to the others that he, or she, is the leader.

Whether appointed beforehand or simply emerging from within the group through some process of natural selection makes little difference. Leaders generally need first to establish, then maintain, the credibility of their position if their leadership is to have a chance of working.

This is most readily seen among children at play, but it occurs in other types of group too, albeit in more subtle ways.

This makes some people think that leaders have a special sort of personality which sets them apart from their followers; that they possess certain qualities and traits which others do not and that this, in the final analysis, is what enables them to lead effectively.

Christ is the supreme example. The Bible records him as saying, on several occasions, 'Follow me.' The commanding force of his personality was such that those to whom he spoke 'left their nets and followed him' (Mt 4:19–20). This happened more than once, to different people in different circumstances, but with the same results.

Attempts to define the special chemistry of a leader's make-up have met with comparatively little success. Endless lists of 'qualities' have been drawn up which often differ from each other because of the requirements of differing situations, and also because they have usually been compiled to emphasise particular viewpoints. The ultimate irony occurs when no sooner has the 'definitive list' been produced, then along comes a leader with a proven track record of success who, much to everyone's chagrin, displays few if any of the qualities on the list!

However, leaders do behave in certain characteristic ways and this does have a lot to do with the way in which their personality is organised. It's best to avoid working from a checklist of qualities like honesty, courage, dependability, tact, persuasiveness, aggressiveness, trustworthiness and so on. The nature of the leadership personality will be better understood if you think of it in terms of the things that flow from it, ie, the outcomes.

So, if you're trying to become a leader or to improve as one, forget about striving to be all the things on your own or someone else's list of personal qualities. Concentrate instead on outcomes.

Ultimately, the effect of the leadership personality is twofold: giving 'direction' and creating 'followership'.

There is a small group of key factors which promote these two important outcomes and which have been found to characterise the behaviour of most practising leaders. More will be said about these in later chapters, but for the moment let's look briefly at each in turn.

The special gifts that make a leader

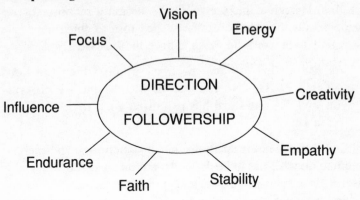

Vision

The capacity to picture the future. All successful leaders have this in common; a penchant for creating and pursuing a vision of the future. George Bernard Shaw, the playwright, remarked: 'Some men see things as they are and say, "Why?" I dream things that never were and say, "Why not?"'

Developing a vision and living it vigorously are essential elements of leadership.

To envision is to take a mental journey from the known into the unknown; it is to arrive at the future and perceive it clearly while still living in the present. Leaders know where they want to get to, they know what they want to achieve. Quite often they will have a clear picture of the end product before knowing how it is to be realised.

It's difficult to imagine anyone leading without this perception. The Bible pictures the likely outcome:

If a blind man leads a blind man, both will fall into a pit (Mt 15:14).

Vision has a compelling effect on the senses. It represents a picture of the preferred future and it promotes the desire to move towards it. Vision gives meaning and purpose to the journey.

The Old Testament leader Moses provides a classic example of this. His vivid picture of God's ultimate purpose for his people, and the intense desire he had to lead them there, are summed up in words he spoke to his father-in-law:

We are setting out for the place about which the Lord said, 'I will give it to you.' Come with us and we will treat you well, for the Lord has promised good things to Israel (Num 10:29).

Vision is that igniting spark that can inspire people and energise them to do what has to be done. An important part of leadership is the capacity to shape and share a vision which gives meaning where meaning is lacking, and which gives point to the endeavours of others.

A later section of this book deals with recognising vision, clarifying it and communicating it. Vision, for the Christian leader, is more than just a bright idea; it goes beyond the creative use of the imagination—it is God-given. The centuries-old words of Paul the apostle make this clear:

No eye has seen, no ear has heard, no mind has conceived what God has prepared for those who love him—but God has revealed it to us by his Spirit (1 Cor 2:9–10).

Focus

The ability to concentrate or focus on issues that are key to the attainment of desired objectives, and subsequently to channel time and effort, together with the necessary resources, in ways that will support the achievement of those objectives.

A rule, known as the 80/20 rule, states: '80% of the "pay-off" comes from 20% of the activities.'

Leaders are good at picking out the '20%' items—sometimes called 'Pareto' items after a nineteenth-century Italian economist, Vilfredo Pareto, who made the observation that 80% of his country's wealth was owned by 20% of the people—and investing in them.

Vision helps keep people focused, energised and on target, but this in itself is not enough. The capacity to focus attention on areas where results are needed, then to develop strategies, draw up plans, allocate resources and orchestrate activities can prove most decisive.

Nehemiah was good at this. His vision of the walls of Jerusalem reconstructed, of community and social life restored, became a reality as a result of his leadership direction. During the high point of activity there were forty-two separate groups at work, each with their work targets clearly defined.

The outcome is expressed in words he penned in his diary afterwards:

So the wall was completed . . . in fifty-two days (Neh 6:15).

Energy

The capacity to act vigorously and decisively; the drive to achieve.

Leaders get results. They finish what they start; they fulfil their mission.

John Wesley, founder of Methodism; William Booth, founder of the Salvation Army; George Müller, founder of that famous orphanage catering for the needs of around 2,000 children for over forty years—they were all 'doers'. They possessed, among other things, a remarkable energy which drove them not only to articulate their respective visions, but to act upon them also.

Jesus, his earthly life drawing to a close, prays confidently to his Father and states:

I have . . . completed the work you gave me to do (Jn 17:4).

Leaders think in terms of accomplishment. One of Henry Ford's pithy statements was: 'You can't build a reputation on what you're going to do.'

The drive to accomplish is an integral part of the leadership personality.

Creativity

The ability to generate ideas; to find creative solutions to problems and generally promote an innovative approach. Leaders are 'possibility thinkers', adept at finding new ways of making progress.

I know of one major company that has struck the word 'problem' from its corporate vocabulary, replacing it with the word 'opportunity'. Employees at all levels are encouraged by this means to think of the potential each situation represents rather than the problem!

The following was written in a prison cell:

I can do everything through him who gives me strength (Phil 4:13).

These words of Paul the apostle reveal something of his approach to life. He did not have a fortress mentality: grimly defensive, simply 'holding the line'. His mode of thinking was positive, creative, expansionist.

Empathy

Sometimes loosely described as 'people skills'. Empathy is the power to project your personality into an object of contemplation and as such it has a wider meaning than the one we're giving it here. However, when viewed in relation to people, this capacity to empathise emerges as a significant component of the leadership personality.

It is a unique kind of insight which allows the leader to see others in total perspective. Those lacking it often fail to read the behavioural clues around them; they look but don't see, listen but don't hear, socialise but don't identify, associate but don't belong.

Some highly intelligent people are almost completely lacking in this area, while others of relatively mediocre ability are intuitively sharp in their judgements of human behaviour.

Empathy is of real importance in leaders. It makes them relate to others effectively. Leaders with empathy know when to talk and when to listen; they are adept at making suggestions because they understand the other person. They are good at sensing discord before it becomes obvious; quick to see when they are on a collision course and able to avert the crash before it occurs.

Influence

The ability to communicate and persuade. Leaders have this faculty. Demosthenes said to his rival orator Aeschines: 'You make them say "How well he speaks." I make them say "Let us march against Philip."'

What is this 'marching magic'—this capacity to move people from the place where they say, 'We know what you mean,' to the place where they say, 'We'll do something about it'?

The ability to influence others is a composite of many factors, but it is a skill which can be developed. More will be said about this in Chapter Four, 'Power and Influence'.

Endurance

The capacity to sustain effort over long periods and keep attention fixed on key issues without becoming distracted.

Moses is described as someone who

persevered because he saw him who is invisible (Heb 11:27).

He had staying power. All successful leaders have this in some measure.

Paul the apostle uses two metaphors which describe his capacity for endurance:

I have fought the good fight, I have finished the race, I have kept the faith (2 Tim 4:8).

This persistent commitment is greatly helped if you have confidence in the vision and its outcomes. Moses and Paul focused their attention on God. They filled their minds with 'right' thoughts. Leaders are continually replaying their vision, rehearsing the outcomes, step by step. Moses was said to be:

looking ahead to his reward (Heb 11:26).

Endurance has more to do with looking ahead than with looking around. Leaders have staying power—they stick to the task.

Stability

The capacity for emotional and mental stability and resilience. It is the kind of thing that keeps the leader steady under pressure, objective under criticism, consistent in behaviour and so on.

This area is mainly concerned with the individual's inner life, and it is the maturity of his or her beliefs and values and attitudes that are central to it.

Alvin Toffler, in his stimulating book *Future Shock*, notes how people who live mobile and stressful lives have what he calls 'stability zones', which enable them to cope with their situations.

One case concerns a man who has changed jobs at a mind-staggering rate, has moved his family thirteen times in eighteen years, travels extensively, uses throw-away products and generally lives in a restless whirl of transience, newness and diversity.

However, a closer look reveals significant stability zones in his life: a good, tightly-woven relationship with his wife of nineteen years; continuing ties with his parents; old college friends interspersed with new acquaintances.

An important way of creating stability zones is through the establishing of routines. It is noteworthy of Jesus that

on the Sabbath day he went into the synagogue, as was his custom (Lk 4:16).

The stability factor in leaders is important. It reflects their capacity for coping with stress, pressure, criticism and adversity.

Faith

A prominent feature of the Christian leader's personality is faith—the capacity to believe. Faith is something all Christians need, but when found in leaders it assumes a special significance because it impinges so much on the task they have to fulfil.

Leaders, by the very nature of their undertaking, are not always in a position to 'play it safe'. They have to be willing to face the unknown at times; to 'walk off the map'. They need the capacity to accept change and adapt to it, and often have to be prepared to take so-called 'risk' decisions when confronted with uncertainty regarding the future.

This boldness to act, far from being a case of 'fools rushing in', comes in fact from a special ingredient of their make-up: faith. It leads to the attainment of goals that might not otherwise have been attempted, far less achieved.

Although all leaders will not possess each of the above gifts to the same degree—the mix will vary from person to person—experience shows that they can be regarded as fairly typical in the personality make-up of most leaders.

Women as leaders

Throughout this book reference is made to leaders as though they were either men or women. No attempt is made to distinguish between the genders as though one were more suited to the role than the other.

Increasingly, nowadays, women are coming to the fore as leaders, often in traditionally male-dominated areas, deploying as they do so their unique blend of perception and skills to good effect.

The Bible contains numerous examples of women in leadership. Miriam, the sister of Moses, appears to have exercised an influential leadership role (Exod 15:20–28); Deborah ruled Israel during the time of the Judges (Judg 4–5); Lydia ran a prayer group (Acts 16:14, 40); Dorcas led a very practical form of charity work (Acts 9:36–43). Outside the Bible itself, there are other case histories which are worth citing: Florence Nightingale, the Lady with the Lamp; Gladys Aylward, who initiated and subsequently led a large-scale missionary enterprise in China; Mother Teresa and her work among the orphans of Calcutta.

A study of the lives of women like these shows them as leaders in their own right. There is little evidence to support the view that they only became leaders by default, ie, because there were no men around who were willing to take on such a role! On the contrary, there is enough evidence to suggest that women are eminently suited to be leaders in a variety of situations.

However, it may be that the way in which women interpret the leadership task and apply themselves to it is unique to their gender, and the importance of this should not be underestimated. Female perceptions of a situation can differ fundamentally from those of the male, as can their approach to key issues like problem-solving. A woman will, quite commonly, tackle a matter in a manner quite different from that of a man. Thought processes, the sense of priorities, action planning and timing can all lead to a different, but no less effective, approach.

The chief thing for consideration by women who aspire to lead is that they should not abandon the essential qualities of their womanhood. Rather, they should recognise the strengths which these represent. Leadership is not a man's job which women can do if they try hard! Failure to recognise this may divert some women into attempting to fulfil the role by doing it as a man would. This is a mistaken action and will result in the uniquely female approach to leadership being jettisoned, with the consequent loss to community or group of that special brand of leadership which only women can exercise.

Women are perfectly capable of exercising leadership in a variety of situations, from the quietly efficient approach of Dorcas in a business setting, to that exercised by Deborah at national level.

However, the context within which women operate as leaders remains significant. More will be said about this in a later chapter.

Why were you chosen?

The answer to this will for ever be something of a mystery. The words of Christ, spoken en route to the Garden of Gethsemane, do little to shed light on the issue.

'You did not choose me' he announced to his disciples, **'but I chose you and appointed you to go and bear fruit' (Jn 15:16).**

We are likely to be much mistaken if we assume that our parentage or our position or the possession of certain attributes qualifies us. The apostle Paul's sweeping generalisation includes leaders:

Brothers think of what you were when you were called. Not many of you were wise by human standards; not many of you were influential; not many of you were of noble birth. But God chose ... foolish things... weak things... lowly things... (1 Cor 1:26–28).

Those whom God chooses he also equips for the task they are to fulfil, and there is a spiritual alchemy at work in the men and women of God's choice which orders their personalities in ways appropriate to their mission. However, though we may understand little of the 'input' side, we can recognise the outcomes.

LEADERSHIP PERSONALITY CHECKLIST

The following checklist may help you to assess how your leadership personality is shaping up.

Consider the factors below and circle a number that most closely represents your view of yourself. Remember that your leadership capability also depends on the situation you are in and on the kind of authority you have. This checklist does not take account of these; it can only act as a guide in helping you to develop an appropriate leadership personality.

	1	2	3	4	
I don't normally think about planning the work of my group. They probably think I'm not a good planner.	1	2	3	4	I always try to plan the work of my group and give the impression I'm a good planner.
I don't usually give the impression that I drive for results. I probably appear indecisive.	1	2	3	4	I am seen as one who drives hard for results by taking quick, decisive action.
I don't spend much time thinking about the future. I take opportunities as they arise. The group have no idea of my view of the future.	1	2	3	4	I have a vision of the future and a plan to get me and my group there. My group are aware of the details.
I am not particularly creative. I rely heavily on my group for ideas.	1	2	3	4	I am very creative, I generate new ideas and my imaginative approach often gets me and the group out of difficulties.
I am not innovative. I prefer the status quo and feel uncomfortable about risks involved in stepping out in faith.	1	2	3	4	I am an innovator with a positive attitude to change. I believe that stepping out in faith can mean taking risks, and I'm prepared for this.
I am weak at communicating with my group. I often have to argue strongly for my ideas and decisions.	1	2	3	4	I communicate well with my group. I can generally influence others to think seriously about my ideas and decisions.

| My group often say they are not involved in decisions and that I don't take their needs into account. | 1 | 2 | 3 | 4 | I involve my group in making decisions. I am seen as being sensitive to others' needs and confident in social situations. |

| Under stress I tend to change my mind and become impatient. I'm probably regarded as inconsistent and moody. | 1 | 2 | 3 | 4 | Under stress I keep a level head and even temper. My behaviour is consistent. I rely on analysing the facts and being fair to people. |

| My capacity for hard work is about average. My enthusiasm does falter on occasions. | 1 | 2 | 3 | 4 | I have a high capacity for hard work. I am always enthusiastic about my work, even in difficult situations. |

Add together the numbers you have circled.

A total of between 27 and 36 shows that you have an effective blend of leadership personality factors.

A total of between 18 and 27 shows that your leadership personality blend is average and that some corrective action is needed.

If the total is between 9 and 18, you have problems with your leadership personality and will need to work at establishing yourself in the eyes of your group. If you are in a leadership position at the moment, then you are very likely trading heavily on the power of your position and relying on the skills and knowledge in your group.

KEY POINTS SUMMARY

Part of the story of leadership—but certainly not the whole story—is the idea that successful leaders have a special sort of personality that separates them from the rest of the herd.

This chapter gives some insight into the make-up of individuals who exercise leadership, and provides a basis for personal assessment and improvement.

The leadership personality has a twofold effect: giving *direction* and creating *followership*.

The behavioural characteristics of leaders are described in terms of nine key factors:

The *vision* factor—ability to create and pursue a vision of the future.

The *focus* or 'directing' factor—ability to organise self and others, and capitalise on effective ways of reaching goals.

The *energy* or 'doing' factor—capacity to act vigorously and decisively; the drive to achieve.

The *creativity* or 'ideas' factor—ability to generate ideas, find creative solutions to problems and generally promote innovative approaches.

The *empathy* or 'people' factor—sensitivity to people, their needs and abilities. Capacity to exercise social and interpersonal skills in a variety of situations.

The *influence* factor—ability to communicate and persuade others.

The *endurance* factor—capacity to sustain effort over long periods and to keep attention focused on key issues without being distracted.

The *stability* factor—ability to maintain emotional stability and resilience. Focus is on the inner life of the individual and on the maturity of his or her beliefs, values and attitudes which enable them to cope with stress, pressure, criticism and adversity.

The *faith* factor—willingness to face the unknown. Capacity to make 'risk' decisions when confronted with the uncertainty of change and the future.

GUIDE FOR ACTION

Look back at your Leadership Personality Checklist and list any factor with a score of 3, 4 or 5. The wording of the factor will give you an insight into the underlying problems. You can improve on these factors by committing yourself to action.

You'll find it helps if you plan your action on three fronts:

- Attitude
- Knowledge
- Skill

A more positive *attitude* will create the context for improvement; more *knowledge* will give you the 'specialist' background you need, and improvements in *skill* will affect the implementation or 'doing' side of what you know.

Another level of insight is in the combination of strong and weak factors. Two critical elements in leadership are the ability of the leader to know where to go and what to do, ie, having direction and being able to motivate others and carry them in the same direction. The first five factors are related to having and giving direction; the last four are related to getting others to follow. Leaders are normally strong in one but weak in the other. Awareness of your general strengths and weaknesses in these areas is important because it highlights a need to integrate one or the other more fully into your leadership personality.

Part Four of this book contains some more helpful ideas for developing a leadership action plan.

Chapter Three

THE LEADERSHIP TASK

Leadership is lifting a personal vision to higher sights, raising a person's performance to a higher standard, building a personality beyond its normal limitations.

Peter Drucker

He tends his flock like a shepherd: He gathers the lambs in his arms and carries them close to his heart; he gently leads those that have young (Is 40:11).

Broadly, the task of leadership is threefold:

- To provide a *vision*.
- To create *teamwork*.
- To *motivate* and *develop* individuals.

Providing vision

The leader's vision, if it is to be realised, must be communicated in convincing ways to everyone who will be affected by it. Then it has to be translated into a set of attainable goals or objectives. These are like milestones or staging posts towards which those directly involved in the process of making the vision a reality can work.

Goal setting takes place in relation to at least five different kinds of work.

Co-ordinating an activity

This is where the achievement of the goal is largely a matter of pulling things together; co-ordinating effort and resources to ensure a specific result, eg, conducting a mission or running a youth camp.

The collection made by Christians living at Antioch for their needy brethren at Jerusalem (Acts 11:29–30)—once the objective was established and agreed—was primarily an exercise in co-ordination.

Cultivating a situation or group

Paul the apostle's description of himself as a 'planter of seed' (1 Cor 3:4) and of Apollos, another Christian leader, as one who 'watered it'—ie, helped to nurture the growing process, highlights a different kind of activity required to achieve an objective. The reference is to a human situation; 'you are God's field' (1 Cor 3:9). We can only guess at what 'planting' and 'watering' implied, but clearly these were activities which were taking place in order to fulfil the aim of maturing, enriching and developing groups of Christians.

Other objectives in this area might include: increasing the level of financial giving within a church and improving relationships between groups of local churches.

Constructing a building

The words of Christ, 'I will build my church' (Mt 16:18), introduce yet another area in which the Christian leader might have objectives to fulfil. Aside from literal building projects, these might include: establishing a library of Christian resource materials and implementing a church growth programme.

Caring for individuals and groups

The Apostle Peter's injunction to 'be shepherds of the flock of God that is under your care' (1 Pet 5:2) can take many forms. Objectives requiring this kind of action could include: establishing a programme of pastoral care and introducing a system of Christian counselling on specific topics.

Caretaking of resources

This might range from introducing a system of financial accounting or a church cleaning programme, to instituting or preserving certain spiritual traditions. The Apostle Paul asked that he and his fellow workers might be regarded as 'those entrusted with the secret things of God' (1 Cor 4:1); the inference being that they were custodians of these things and therefore responsible for their proper use.

Creating teams and promoting teamwork

Much of what you want to achieve as a leader depends upon the co-operation and efforts of others, and for this reason the need to create teams and promote teamwork is often crucial.

A team is 'a group of people who share common objectives and who need to work together to achieve them'.

A team can accomplish much more than the sum of its individual members, and yet groups of people are often seen to achieve less than could have been accomplished by individuals working alone.

Teamwork is about what happens when the team works. Teamwork is individuals working together and accomplishing more than they could on their own.

One of the simplest ways of seeing the difference between teams and teamwork is to think of two football teams; both have eleven players and both are teams, yet one may be constantly winning matches while the other is not. The difference is a matter of teamwork.

A similar effect can be seen within churches and Christian organisations. The apostle's appeal for unity (1 Cor 1:10–11) underscores the importance of teamwork in this context:

I beseech you. . . that ye be perfectly joined together in the same mind and in the same judgment (AV).

When people are together in harmony, their effectiveness as an achieving group is greatly enhanced. The social effects should not go unnoticed either. It's good to be part of a successful team.

Behold, how good and how pleasant it is for brethren to dwell together in unity. . . there the Lord commanded the blessing, even life for evermore (Ps 133:1, 3 AV).

Teams of people are like individuals—they have a group personality and character which is unique to themselves. Group personality is an important factor in terms of the team's capacity to function effectively and achieve results. It takes time for this to form, but the leader can and should influence its development to a significant degree.

There are four stages of team development and it is useful to understand these; first, because there is every likelihood that you'll have to work with an undeveloped team at some stage in your leadership career and second, an awareness of how teams typically develop will help you to appreciate why your group—if it happens to be an established one—got to be like it now is!

The four stages are:

- Forming
- Storming
- Norming
- Performing

Forming

During this stage the group has no established way of working. People will be uncertain about how to tackle the task and about each other. Individuals will begin to assert themselves and one or two may try to impose their ideas. Every group goes through this stage; the forming process is key to future performance.

Storming

During this stage a considerable amount of conflict and disagreement may surface as the group sorts itself out. Sometimes this disagreement is suppressed and emotions contained; this is not a good thing because group character and behavioural norms are beginning to evolve, and if hidden agendas are allowed to remain and grievances are secretly nursed, the group will suffer in the longer term.

It should be noted that some groups never succeed in getting past this stage. . .

Norming

This is the stage where consensus is reached. Initially this may be simply about how the group ought to work. Agreement over the way decisions are taken usually takes longer to achieve since these are based on shared values. Sometimes a group will go too far at this stage and, in a reaction to the disagreements and comparative chaos of the 'forming' and 'storming' stages, may take refuge in formal procedures and systems.

Performing

This describes the smoothly functioning team. The change from 'norming' to 'performing' is often marked by the replacement of formal systems with trust and strong informal relationships.

Effective teams are characterised by the following:

- Success: High performing teams achieve what they set out to do.
- Clear objectives: These are consistent with the organisation of which the team is part and are also accepted by the team members. This is almost always the starting point for improving the performance of any team.
- Balanced individual roles: Roles are clear, they support the team effort and are agreed by those who carry them out. In addition to roles that are related to the specific tasks which team members have, it is important for leaders to recognise that there are three basic types of team member.
- Communication: In a good team this is open, honest and continuous.
- Growth: The group learns and develops in effectiveness.

- Relationships: Within the team these are supportive, trusting and strong enough to withstand the healthy conflict and argument which properly functioning teams contain.

Promoting team development

Three key issues affect the proper development of teams and lead to the characteristics mentioned above.

Direction

Of all the factors which can destroy a team quickly, the chiefest is lack of direction. Teams rely heavily on the leader to establish objectives and the general direction to be taken. When these are unclear, then team members will develop their own and these may become the subject of disagreement among the other members.

Involvement

Teams work well because they produce better decisions than any individual in the team. Participation in the process is important.

Harmony

The spirit of harmony leads to better team performance. This unity of purpose and endeavour has to be distinguished from mere uniformity, which is often just a cosmetic form of unity and may be quite unreal.

These three factors are probably the most critical in developing strong and consistent teamwork. Here are a few practical hints which will help bring them about:

- Work with the team to establish a clear statement of its objectives.
- Try to ensure that the discussion is well managed. Establish *facts* first, then move on to *interpretation*, and finally agree on *conclusions*.
- Develop a team atmosphere where feelings can be expressed

and members feel closely involved in the decision-making process.

- Seek harmony. Co-operate with your team; don't compete. Avoid giving them an ultimatum—they'll react to it and you negatively. Never vote to resolve a conflict; talk it through, however much you may feel you're wasting valuable time!

Teams represent unique opportunities to make things happen which might not otherwise occur. For example:

- Co-ordination of individual efforts.
- Generation of commitment.
- Provision of support and help to members.
- Meeting a basic human need to belong.
- Enhancing communication.
- Provision of learning opportunities.

There are at least five types of team to be found in a church or Christian organisation:

The top team

Sometimes called the 'ministry team', 'oversight', 'presbytery' or 'Executive Committee'. Generally, the main roles of the top team are to:

- Envision the future.
- Decide the direction of the church or organisation.
- Develop strategy.
- Identify key opportunities to be pursued.
- Clarify values.
- Decide what the church or organisation stands for.
- Oversee operations.
- Authorise major decisions.
- Resolve conflicts between different functions.
- Design and develop the organisation.

- Appoint people to key positions.
- Maintain high-level contacts with other people and/or other churches or organisations in the outside world.

Management teams

Sometimes called 'Diaconate', 'Board of Deacons', 'Management Committee' or 'Parish Council'. They co-ordinate and control the work of others. They provide the day-to-day leadership. They relate to the main body of church members or of the organisation. They allocate resources, plan operations and, ideally, manage the boundaries between different functions.

Operator teams

These are the people who get the job done, eg, a group of Sunday school teachers; a group dedicated to maintenance of the church's physical assets; an intercessory prayer group.

Specialist/support teams

These provide the specialist support needed to get the job done. They may be groups of people whose ministry or work associates them, eg, house groups, musicians, art and drama specialists, counsellors and outreach teams.

Often these groups facilitate the setting of standards within the church or organisation, ensuring a uniform approach or the promotion of issues that are seen as key.

Project teams

Sometimes called 'task groups'. These may consist of separate groups brought together for specific purposes, eg, to deal with a building project, conduct an evangelistic mission or some other one-off event.

There are many examples throughout the New Testament which

show teams of the above sort to have been in existence.

The twelve apostles represented a top team:

The Twelve gathered all the disciples together and said, 'It would not be right for us to neglect the ministry of the word of God in order to wait on tables' (Acts 6:2).

They appointed an operator team:

Choose seven men from among you...We will turn this responsibility over to them (Acts 6:3).

There is some evidence that these seven appointees became a management team in their own right with responsibility for other operator and specialist teams, notably Philip whose forte was evangelism.

In Acts 13:1–2 there is evidence of a specialist team at work:

In the church at Antioch there were prophets and teachers... While they were worshipping the Lord and fasting, the Holy Spirit said, 'Set apart for me Barnabas and Saul for the work to which I have called them.' So they...placed their hands on them and sent them off.

This diagram shows how different teams and their leaders might be grouped within a local church.

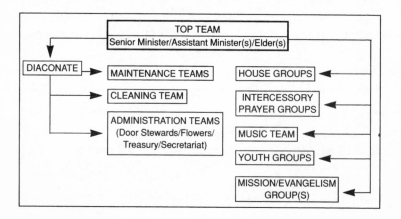

Developing and motivating individuals

Every team is made up of individuals, and the success of the team depends to a large extent on the way in which those individuals support and work with each other. The need to *develop* and *motivate* individuals is a third component of the leadership task.

Concern over the performance of a team member led to a split in the working relationship between Paul and Barnabas.

Some time later Paul said to Barnabas, 'Let us go back and visit the brothers in all the towns where we preached the word of the Lord and see how they are doing.' Barnabas wanted to take John, also called Mark, with them, but Paul did not think it wise to take him because he had deserted them in Pamphylia and had not continued with them in the work. They had such a sharp disagreement that they parted company (Acts 15:36-39).

Who was right—Paul or Barnabas?

When the performance of an individual team member isn't up to scratch, what do you do? One answer is to drop them from the team. Or you could arrange for them to be moved into a situation which matches their talents and abilities better. Sometimes this is the only answer and may be the kindest thing to do; some square pegs have a habit of defying every effort to make them fit round holes.

However, before resorting to such Draconian methods you could try developing and motivating the person concerned. It is necessary to have a certain amount of faith in people; to be willing to invest something of yourself in them and maybe take a few risks. We don't have enough information to judge whether Paul or Barnabas was right here, but certainly either option can be the correct answer.

Individuals, including the ones who are performing well, need support and opportunities for growth. Barnabas appears to have given John Mark the encouragement and support he needed at that time, and as a consequence, the man destined to be the author of the second Gospel proved that failure need not be final.

These three concerns of leadership, namely: *providing a vision* which can be translated into attainable goals, *creating teams and promoting teamwork* and *developing and motivating* individuals, can be represented diagrammatically, like this:

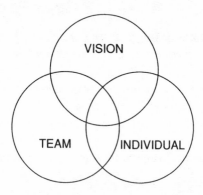

Three intersecting circles show the inter-relationship there is between the attainment of a particular goal or objective, the performance of the team involved and the contribution of individual team members. The leader's task is to give synergy to the forces at work in these three areas.

This model was first developed by Professor John Adair as the cornerstone of his Action-Centred leadership approach. It depicts the three major components of any leadership situation. Christian leaders, regardless of the type of objective they are targeting or the type of team they are leading, can conveniently think of their task in this way.

Within this framework, the specifics of any leadership task, whether running a church, organising a March for Jesus event or leading a youth group, can be itemised as a series of clearly-defined actions which have to be performed if the group is to work as a team, the objective is to be realised and individual development and motivation is to take place.

There are eight functions or actions of leadership which can be identified in this way:

Define objectives

Objectives should be CLEAR. You can't hit a target you can't see. One way to clarify objectives is to make them specific, that is, capable of being measured. This is easier when the objective lies in an area where things are quantifiable, as in the case of improving church attendance. It is more difficult to be specific where the aim is to improve relationships between church members. But one way might be to look for an increase in the numbers attending, say, church family days or other purely social events.

Objectives should be CORRECT, that is, they should serve the vision or mission purpose.

Objectives should be REALISTIC, that is, capable of being achieved; it should be possible to plan for their attainment.

As well as goal- or task-related objectives there are those which have to be defined in relation to the group, for example, its size, membership and development needs, and to individual members, for example, their motivation, skills development, well being and so on.

The leader has to keep these in scope as he or she specifies the targets for attainment.

Develop strategies

Objectives, however well defined, are unlikely to be achieved unless accompanied by carefully ordered plans. There is truth in the saying: 'If you fail to plan, you plan to fail.'

Strategies must be developed which take due account of the key factors influencing the situation and which bring the necessary resources to bear on it with the right degree of timing.

The words of Paul the apostle serve as a reminder that the action God takes in support of his purposes is premeditated:

When the time had fully come, God sent his Son, born of a woman, born under law, to redeem those under law, that we might receive the full rights of sons (Gal 4:4–5).

God is working to a plan. His actions are programmed to take effect with precise timing.

The characteristics of a good strategy are:

Flexibility—being capable of accepting change. There is a slightly cynical view which suggests that the only thing about a plan which can be guaranteed is that it won't work! It's not possible to predict everything with certainty. The unforeseen nearly always happens and for that reason plans should be made adaptable. A good way of ensuring this is to ask, 'In how many ways could this plan fail?' Then build in the necessary contingency arrangements where you can to meet the crises, if and when they arise.

Controllability. This follows flexibility. How will you make sure things go according to plan? And when they don't, how will you know? What monitoring arrangements are in place which will signal any unacceptable deviations in time for you to take corrective action?

Simplicity. The simpler the plan or strategy, the easier it will be to communicate, implement, control and, where necessary, adapt.

Communicate

Plans, once developed, have to be communicated to those who are required to put them into effect. People need information, instruction and, in lots of cases, inspiration to allow them to get on with the job and each other.

Briefing and, if needed, training come first. Objectives and plans for attaining them need explanation. Individual roles have to be made clear, along with results expected and the kind of support available.

Team briefings, individual counselling sessions and progress reporting are all features of the leader's communication programme.

Control

This means having standards and sticking to them. These standards may take the form of performance targets, procedures or personal values. The leader monitors progress, measures results and makes corrections, where necessary, to stay on course. He or she has to be in control, making things happen instead of simply letting them happen.

This is essential if objectives are to be realised, the team is to remain effective and individuals are to stay in tune with the entire process.

Evaluate

There is an incident recorded in Matthew's Gospel which illustrates the need to evaluate people and things correctly.

While Jesus was in Bethany in the home of a man known as Simon the Leper, a woman came to him with an alabaster jar of very expensive perfume, which she poured on his head as he was reclining at the table. When the disciples saw this, they were indignant. 'Why this waste?' they asked. 'This perfume could have been sold at a high price and the money given to the poor' (Mt 26:6–9).

The disciples of Jesus, concerned as they were about the extension of Christ's kingdom, evaluated this woman's action as having little worth. Jesus, however, perceived the situation in a different light. He saw what she had done as a valuable contribution to what they were about, and allowed it to stand.

Leaders are constantly having to make judgements about the situations they are in; checking the feasibility of ideas, assessing the worth of somebody's contribution, evaluating the benefits and drawbacks of different courses of action before choosing between them.

People as they act, situations as they develop, all have to be assessed against their likely impact on the attainment of objectives, the working of the group as a whole and the performance of individuals.

Motivate

It is hard to think of a leader who does not motivate others. The words 'motive' and 'motivation' come from a Latin verb meaning 'to move'. What moves people to act may come from within themselves or from some external pressure, or—more commonly—from a combination of both.

Motivation has to do with what happens within individuals in terms of wanting to do something and also with what happens outside of them as they are influenced by others or by circum-stances. When the leader is motivating someone, he or she is consciously or unconsciously trying to change the strength and direction of that person's motive energy. The same thing applies in the case of groups, although the process is more complicated.

The aim of motivation is to influence the behaviour of individuals or groups so that the organisation will function effectively.

Motivation has to be distinguished from manipulation. To manipulate someone implies controlling them by artful or unfair means, especially when it's to your advantage. Motivating others therefore should not be confused with the manipulatory practices used by strong personalities to dominate weaker ones.

Organise

People, as individuals and also as groups, need a structure within which they can work. In this context the concept of organising goes beyond that of merely ensuring that the right people, facilities, physical resources and so on are brought together with proper timing and support. The leader has to think about the kind of structure he or she wants the organisation to have so that it will best meet the demands placed upon it. Organising is about creating relationships of the working, reporting, supporting kind, as well as providing resources.

Organisational development is a topic of particular significance for those leaders who have overall responsibility for large churches which may consist of many sub-groups of people, or large, complex Christian organisations. In lots of instances, not only has the 'one man band' been replaced by the 'ministry team' approach, but the organisation's infrastructure has changed too, and this is reflected by the shift from hierarchies, with their pecking orders and the subsequent emphasis on authorising and reporting procedures, to networks of groups which have greater autonomy and where the emphasis is on inter-relationships; the 'body' concept. These terms will be described in more detail later. At this stage it is important to register that one of the main components of the leadership task is organising.

The leader has to determine what he or she wants the organisation to become in terms of its size, shape and way of working so that it can accommodate change and be a vehicle for implementing change and achieving results.

Exemplify

Setting an example is a key requirement of the leadership task. Paul the apostle urges Timothy, the young leader of the church at Ephesus, to

set an example for the believers in speech, in life, in love, in faith and in purity (1 Tim 4:12).

We might paraphrase these words as, 'Be worth imitating,' or, 'Be a role model.'

These eight functions describe the mechanics of the leadership task. By concentrating on these, leaders will find themselves doing the things which are necessary for meeting the objectives, moulding the team and making it work and developing and motivating individual team members.

Noticeably, the foregoing fall into two categories: *starting* activities and *continuing* activities.

Defining objectives and planning are most closely connected with getting things going. The remainder are more linked to the job of keeping things going. Typically, a good leader will work hard at getting things underway, but when the team is working well, change to a different mode of operating by reducing day-to-day involvement with the task and increasing overall, general leadership of the team and its direction. We describe this as the 'helicopter' approach—getting away from the close-up picture and seeing the whole job from a distance.

LEADERSHIP TASK CHECKLIST

Here is a matrix of test questions with scores which will help you to assess your current strengths, weaknesses and preferences in relation to managing the leadership task and which will provide you with a basis for making personal improvements.

Consider the factors below and circle a number that most closely represents your view of yourself.

I spend little time defining the task. Generally, the team and I define it as we go along.	1	2	3	4	I spend a lot of time defining the task and ensuring that the team understand it.
Normally I have a sketchy plan to start with. The rest of it evolves as the team and I proceed.	1	2	3	4	I believe that any task needs a sound plan. I also think the team should be involved in the planning process.

	1	2	3	4	
A common complaint in my team is that some members don't know what the others are expected to achieve or what activities are being pursued.	1	2	3	4	When an action plan has been developed I spend time ensuring that all team members know everyone else's objectives and activities.
I find I have to check constantly on what's being done or achieved. Often I have to redirect people.	1	2	3	4	I control the task effectively by ensuring that each team member is in full control of their work.
I often find myself too involved in the task and I lack time to spot problems ahead of the team's work.	1	2	3	4	Once the team is working well I look ahead to spot problems that may arise.
I rely on team members' own motivation to achieve the task.	1	2	3	4	I spend time motivating team members.
I rarely spend time ensuring that the team is organised. I rely on its own ability to communicate and to ensure delegation throughout the organisation.	1	2	3	4	I keep an eye on the organisation of the team. I stimulate communication among members and I make sure authority is well delegated throughout the organisation.
I rarely think about the impact of my example on the team.	1	2	3	4	I am always aware of the need to set the right example. Generally, I try to 'do' and 'be' what I expect in others.

When you've circled a number for each factor, add the numbers together. If you have a total between 24 and 32 you are probably quite good at managing the leadership process.

If you have a total between 16 and 24 then there is scope for you to improve the way you manage the leadership process. You can make progress by being more specific about improving your process skills. Your team members are probably having to rely too heavily at present on their own strengths to achieve for the team as a whole.

If you have a total between 8 and 16 you are particularly weak at managing the process. Your team is definitely achieving in spite of you rather than because of you.

KEY POINTS SUMMARY

The purpose of this chapter is to provide a clear picture of what leaders do and to help you form action plans which relate to the situations you face.

Key components of the leadership scenario are described as:

- The task/mission to be accomplished.
- The people who are to accomplish it:
    As a group which has to be maintained
    As individuals who have to be developed and supported.

Five key biblical areas where Christian leaders may have to establish goals are identified and described, namely:

- Co-ordinating activities
- Cultivating activities
- Constructing activities
- Caring activities
- Caretaking activities

The duties and responsibilities of leaders are identified in terms of eight tasks or functions:

- Defining objectives
- Developing strategies
- Communicating
- Controlling
- Evaluating
- Motivating
- Organising
- Setting an example

The functions of leadership are outlined in relation to two key requirements: *starting* activities and *continuing* activities.

GUIDE FOR ACTION

Identify the kind of team or group you lead:

- Top team
- Management team
- Operator team
- Specialist/support team
- Project team

List the areas in which your goals or tasks generally lie:

- Co-ordination work
- Cultivation work
- Construction work
- Caring work
- Caretaking work

Look back at your Leadership Task Checklist and list any factors with a score of 1 or 2. Again, the wording of the factor will give you some insight into the underlying problem(s).

Normally, weakness in managing the leadership process is due to a lack of awareness of the need to manage it. Now that this awareness has been highlighted by the text and the checklist, you need to make a specific commitment to managing your next leadership task more effectively.

Think through the task and decide how you're going to:

- Define
- Plan
- Communicate
- Control
- Evaluate
- Motivate
- Organise
- Set an example

Make notes about your thinking and commit yourself to putting your ideas into action when the time is right.

Another level of insight can be gained by studying the combination of the factors. The first three factors are related to *getting things started*.

The others are about *keeping things going*. Good leaders can 'change gear', switching from day-to-day close involvement with things in order to get them going, to taking a more strategic overview when the work is underway. Balance between these two stances is important.

Part Four of this book has some further helpful suggestions for improvement.

PART TWO

Developing an Effective Style

The true leader must always be able to disillusion.

'No Rusty Swords'—Dietrich Bonhoeffer

The good leader needs to work hard at strategising, mobilising and inspiring. But the leader also needs to help people gain a more realistic view of his role and abilities. A leader who feeds his ego on the larger-than-life adulation of his followers is a danger to himself and to others.

A leader needs to delegate, acknowledge weakness and disbelieve other people's myths about him. Moreover, he needs to see his position as a privileged responsibility and not as an inherent right.

Meditation: The good leader has a true perspective on his position, role and task, as well as his responsibility and shortcomings.

Chapter Four

POWER AND INFLUENCE

Obey your leaders and submit to their authority (Heb 13:17).

Power tends to corrupt, and absolute power corrupts absolutely.

Lord Acton

Words like 'power' and 'influence' do not rest easily in the minds of some Christians, especially when they appear in the context of Christian leadership. They conjure unwelcome images of people acquiring too much control in certain circumstances and perhaps using it unwisely or selfishly.

Too much power, too much influence, is unhealthy as can be seen in the case of one early Christian leader, roundly criticised by the Apostle John for his high-handed manner and domineering ways:

Diotrephes, who loves to be first, will have nothing to do with us. So if I come, I will call attention to what he is doing, gossiping maliciously about us. Not satisfied with that, he refuses to welcome the brothers. He also stops those who want to do so and puts them out of the church (3 Jn 9–10).

Even so, the fact remains that power and influence play an indispensable part in the leadership process. Coming to terms with this may be difficult, but it has to be done from the outset if the process is to be understood.

Influence is the means by which one person modifies the attitudes, behaviour and actions of others. Power is what enables him or her to do it. Influence is a process; power—the ability to influence—is a resource.

By definition, the leader of a group has to possess some kind of power. Whether this is given, generated or simply 'grabbed' is immaterial. Without it, he or she cannot exert any real leadership influence, regardless of the techniques or methods they choose to adopt.

Leadership has to do with the exercise of power, and all leaders—including Christian leaders, whether bishops, pastors of churches, Sunday school superintendents or leaders of house groups—have, by virtue of the roles they are expected to fulfil, a significant amount of power vested in them. Leadership is what determines how much of it will be realised.

Sources of power

God is the ultimate source of all power. Referring to magistrates, rulers and others in positions of authority, the Apostle Paul says:

> **Everyone must submit himself to the governing authorities, for there is no authority except that which God has established. The authorities that exist have been established by God (Rom 13:1).**

Pontius Pilate discovered this when, during the trial of Jesus, he said to him:

> **Don't you realise I have power either to free you or to crucify you?**

To which Jesus replied:

> **You would have no power over me if it were not given to you from above (Jn 19:10–11).**

The fact that God is the ultimate source of power is again highlighted in the words of the Great Commission which Jesus later gave to his disciples:

All authority in heaven and on earth has been given to me. Therefore go. . . (Mt 28:18–19).

Every servant of Christ can lay claim to this delegated power as he goes about his Master's business. The Christian leader is no exception; he can act with Christ's authority as in his name.

This does not imply that leaders have a divine right to do as they please. Quite the reverse. The Christian who does not maintain a vital link with Christ is helpless; powerless to achieve anything.

Jesus uses the allegory of the vine and its branches to explain the significance of this to his followers:

I am the vine; you are the branches. . .apart from me you can do nothing (Jn 15:5).

The keys to maintaining this vital relationship are:

- The action of the *word* of God in the Christian (Jn 15:3, 7).
- The practice of *prayer* (Jn 15:7).
- Continual *obedience* to Christ's commands (Jn 15:10, 14).

Christian leaders need to experience the power of God if they are to be effective in fulfilling their roles. Fellowship with Christ is the means to obtaining and maintaining it. Without it the leader is nothing more than an organiser of human effort and activity. With it he is a tool in the hands of God to accomplish his purposes on earth.

That said, there are four major areas where this leadership power seems to be generated. For the Christian leader these may be regarded, in a secondary sense, as sources of power. The diagram which follows illustrates these four areas.

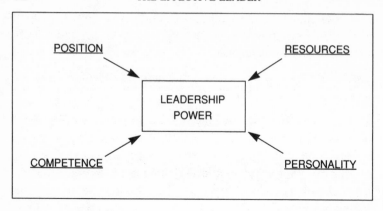

Position power

Leaders can have a certain amount of power, simply because of the position they hold within their organisation. It comes with the job.

The Roman Centurion who came to Jesus for help described it in the simplest of terms:

> **I myself am a man under authority, with soldiers under me. I tell this one, 'Go,' and he goes; and that one, 'Come,' and he comes. I say to my servant, 'Do this,' and he does it (Mt 8:9).**

This is position power and it is the least subtle, most readily understood form of authority. Perhaps you've heard the expression 'pulling rank'. It refers to those occasions when someone has used their superior position or status to exert their influence in a given situation.

Using your position in this way is a bit like wielding a blunt instrument: wise leaders invoke the authority invested in their position only as a last resort.

Personal power

There is a degree of authority which some people possess because of the way in which they are able to project their personality. The word 'charismatic' is often used to describe them and it's important not to underestimate this capacity. Authority which stems from the personality is common within organisations. Even those who don't hold official positions can still exert a powerful leadership influence because of their personal charisma.

Personal power has another dimension; it relates to the character of the individual concerned. Think of someone who shows consistency of purpose and of action; who has a reputation for being dependable and trustworthy. Such a person has the potential to influence others because of what they are in themselves. The key word that describes this is 'integrity'.

People are extremely responsive to this kind of leader. But it has its down side. The Apostle Peter, whose personal qualities virtually guaranteed him a following, had to learn that his enthusiasm did not always reflect the will of God. The building project he had in mind following the marvellous scenes witnessed on the Mount of Transfiguration had to be halted, promptly (Mt 17:1–5). Again, soon after the resurrection of Christ, his plan to go fishing led him and the others who followed him into a night of fruitless endeavour (Jn 21:1–6).

Expert power

This is a matter of competence. Experience, expertise, 'know-how', when related to the work in hand, can provide a base for leadership authority. The person who knows what to do, or who has information which others do not have, will often find themselves in a position to lead.

An old proverb wisely observes: 'In the country of the blind, the one-eyed man is King.'

Resource power

This occurs when someone has resources that are needed by the others. For example, children playing a game that involves the use of a bat and ball sometimes find that the owner of these items can get his own way by threatening to remove the bat and ball and thereby stop the game! This individual can control what happens, to a certain extent, because they control the resources.

This is resource power!

On a more serious note, the possession of needed funds or facilities can create a power base for the owner, if he or she so wishes. Resources don't have to be material; they can be the capacity to give someone a job or provide opportunities to speak to groups and so on.

Needless to say, this kind of power only works if the person using it has control of the resources and if those resources really are wanted.

Leadership power—that mysterious capacity to influence others—is drawn in the main from the above 'sources'. In some instances it can be seen that an individual is relying almost solely on one strength, eg, personality. But in most cases, the leader's forcefulness stems from a combination of all four.

In summary, the Christian leader's source of power might be represented diagrammatically, like this:

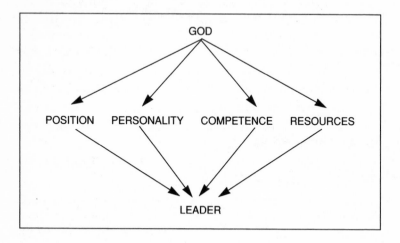

Methods of influence

There are four main ways of exerting influence:

Coercion or force

It is perfectly possible to get people to do things by putting them under pressure. Those with position or resource power can do it. The means need not be physical. There are other, more sophisticated ways. Withholding resources is one way; another is to make use of rules and procedures.

A good example concerns the case of Daniel, who lived during the despotic reign of Darius, King of the Medes and Persians (Dan 5:31). Daniel held a key position in the king's administration to the extent that his colleagues in government were extremely jealous of him. They plotted against him for a while, unsuccessfully, before finally resorting to the clever use of rules and procedures—for which their system was renowned— in order to bring him down.

> **So the administrators and the satraps went as a group to the king and said: 'O King Darius, live for ever! The royal administrators, prefects, satraps, advisers and governors have all agreed that the king should issue an ediçt and enforce the decree that anyone who prays to any god or man during the next thirty days, except to you, O king shall be thrown into the lions' den. Now, O king, issue the decree and put it in writing so that it cannot be altered—in accordance with the laws of the Medes and Persians, which cannot be repealed.' So King Darius put the decree in writing (Dan 6:6–9).**

Circumscribing a situation with rules and procedures is one way of influencing the behaviour of whole groups of people who happen to be in that situation. However, the target in this case was not the entire population of Darius' kingdom but a single individual within it: Daniel. His prayer habits were widely known, as was the strength of his religious conviction. This rule was carefully framed and introduced, knowing that it would bring Daniel into conflict with the king who would then be forced to move against him.

Now when Daniel learned that the decree had been published, he went home to his upstairs room where the windows opened towards Jerusalem. Three times a day he got down on his knees and prayed, giving thanks to his God, just as he had done before. Then these men went as a group and found Daniel praying and asking God for help. So they went to the king and spoke to him about his royal decree... Then they said to the king, 'Daniel, who is one of the exiles from Judah, pays no attention to you, O king, or to the decree you put in writing. He still prays three times a day.' When the king heard this, he was greatly distressed; he was determined to rescue Daniel and made every effort until sundown to save him. Then the men went as a group to the king and said to him, 'Remember, O king, that according to the law of the Medes and Persians no decree or edict that the king issues can be changed.' So the king gave the order and they brought Daniel and threw him into the lions' den (Dan 6:10–16).

This represents the tactical use of influence. It's a form of politics by which a person or group of persons can influence another to do something through the skilful and highly selective use of procedures, new or existing. By this means people are able to get their own way while appearing to stay within the rules.

The religious Pharisees regularly used this tactic, strictly observing the letter of God's law, but at the same time often conveniently ignoring the spirit and intention of that law, simply using it as a device to establish their position and impose their will on others.

One instance concerns an occasion when they tried to undermine the authority of Christ by challenging him about the conduct of his disciples on the Sabbath day:

One Sabbath Jesus was going through the cornfields, and as his disciples walked along, they began to pick some ears of corn. The Pharisees said to him, 'Look, why are they doing what is unlawful on the Sabbath?' (Mk 2:23–24).

Technically, the challenge was correct. But the influence attempt failed. In his reply, Jesus quoted case law, reminding them of what the great King David and his companions did when they were hungry and in need. But the *piece de resistance* is contained in a superb statement which Jesus makes right at the end of the exchange:

> **Then he said to them, 'The Sabbath was made for man, not man for the Sabbath. So the Son of Man is Lord even of the Sabbath' (Mk 2:27).**

Rules and procedures are necessary. No society, organisation or group can function effectively without them. Sometimes, the leader has no option but to invoke the authority of his or her position and insist on a course of action, be it according to the rules or otherwise. This takes courage since the leader may be under pressure to back off. In situations like this, leaders not only need to be convinced that their cause is right, but also that their personal position is reasonably secure and that they have the necessary resources to implement their decision and see it through successfully.

Clearly there is more to Christian leadership than merely laying down the law and making sure that everyone sticks by it. The use of force, by whatever means, as a way of influencing others, is generally regarded as a short-term tactic which can have disastrous longer-term effects. The minister who insists that his people do certain things in certain ways, simply because it is his wish that they should, may get people's compliance, provided he has the will to enforce his wishes and is in a position to do so, but he will not necessarily gain their commitment and may have to face an unwelcome backlash later.

Persuasion

This is usually the method of first resort. It relies on the power of argument and the evidence of facts. The leader with expert knowledge or experience in certain areas can often persuade others to follow. For example, the pioneer evangelist who has been successful in establishing churches is likely to be able to persuade others to go along with his ideas in a new situation because his track record in that area shows his competence.

Persuasion has another aspect. This has less to do with the ability to present a convincing case based on arguing from facts or experience than with the capacity of the leader to project his or her personality. Personal magnetism, the pull of a stronger force, sometimes accounts for it. Most of us have felt at times the almost inexplicable attraction of another person and the accompanying desire to follow them and work for them. This kind of thing depends on personal, and sometimes expert, power. Trust, respect, charm, enthusiasm: these are some of the things that allow the leader to influence others without seeming to impose upon them.

They don't have to persuade in the conventional sense, or give reasons. People are simply drawn to them, convinced of their ability, or their principles, even their loyalty. This feeling of being pulled towards someone, in its strongest form love, can influence people to abandon their rationality. The Apostle Paul alludes to it in one of his letters:

If we are out of our mind, it is for the sake of God; if we are in our right mind, it is for you. For Christ's love compels us, because we are convinced that one died for all, and therefore all died. And he died for all, that those who live should no longer live for themselves but for him who died for them and was raised again (2 Cor 5:13–15).

Reward

It may be claimed, with some justification, that this is a way of influencing. Leaders who have the necessary resource power can influence the behaviour of others by offering the right kind of incentive. It is possible for this to degenerate into a form of bribery—simply using, or not using, resources in order to obtain a desired response. This is manipulation.

However, the intelligent use of rewards as a means of

encouraging and developing the right kind of actions in people is perfectly legitimate as a method of exerting influence. A keen understanding of people, including their needs and aspirations in particular situations, is crucial to success when using this method. For example, someone may need recognition while the main concern of someone else may be for security. Again, there are others who are perhaps looking for fulfilment of some sort.

Jesus, during his great discourse on the Bread of Life, makes an astonishing statement about himself:

> **'Whoever eats my flesh and drinks my blood remains in me, and I in him. Just as the living Father sent me and I live because of the Father, so the one who feeds on me will live because of me.'** ...**On hearing it, many of his disciples said, 'This is a hard teaching. Who can accept it?' (Jn 6:56–57, 60).**

His influence attempt—that is, persuasion using words—had failed.

> **From this time many of his disciples turned back and no longer followed him (Jn 6:66).**

Jesus then turns to the Twelve and asks:

> **You do not want to leave me too, do you? (Jn 6:67).**

The answer is most revealing. Peter, the spokesman, replies:

> **Lord, to whom shall we go? You have the words of eternal life (Jn 6:68).**

This is resource power at work—the capacity to give them what they needed and wanted. This is one reason why many people continue to belong to a certain group or church. It is not a mere tradition or a sense of duty. There are plenty of other churches around, but they keep going to this one because they gain something from attending which they feel they might not find if they went elsewhere.

Needs and aspirations vary from person to person and may

even change within each individual over time, as their personal circumstances alter. More will be said about this later. At this stage it is sufficient to note that if rewarding people is to work as a method of influence, the rewards must be appropriate to the needs of the individual.

Example

People can be influenced not only by what they hear, but by seeing what others do. The advice of the Apostle Paul to one New Testament leader underscores this as a powerful means of influence:

Set an example for the believers in speech, in life, in love, in faith and in purity (1 Tim 4:12).

People respond more readily to actions than to words, and the challenge laid before every Christian leader is that they be 'worth imitating'.

There is a quaint rhyme that begins: 'I'd rather see a sermon than hear one any day.' This hints at the power of example; the capacity not only to explain, but to compel others to act in the same way. It is the latter which constitutes example as a means of influence, and that's what makes it important to leaders.

One of the main lessons to be learned from categorising sources of power and methods of influence in this way is in seeing the relationship between them and in recognising that influence methods are only as effective as their power sources. To increase in influence, the leader has to work on these sources and nourish them carefully. Take, for instance, the matter of trust; this is a key component of many power/influence scenarios. Yet trust is often like a pane of glass—put one foot wrong and it is quickly shattered and may be difficult to repair.

Using these categories, a typical relationship might look like this:

Method of influence	Power source required
Coercion/Force	Position Power Resource Power Personal Power
Persuasion	Expert Power Personal Power
Example	Personal Power
Reward	Resource Power Position Power

Choosing the right method of influence

Suppose you want to decide the most appropriate way of influencing a situation. Before you do so, three other things have to be taken into account.

First, there is the *credibility* of your authority in the eyes of those you are trying to influence. How do they perceive you? For example, you may think you have expert power, but they might not see you in that way at all.

Consider the case of the seven sons of Sceva:

Some Jews who went around driving out evil spirits tried to invoke the name of the Lord Jesus over those who were demon-possessed. They would say, 'In the name of Jesus, whom Paul preaches, I command you to come out.' Seven sons of Sceva, a Jewish chief priest, were doing this. The evil spirit answered them, 'Jesus I know, and Paul I know about, but who are you?' Then the man who had the evil spirit jumped on them and overpowered them all. He gave them such a beating that they ran out of the house naked and bleeding (Acts 19:13–16).

This was an attempt by seven well-intentioned men to influence a situation by using force, but who found themselves unable to do it because they lacked the necessary authority or position power.

Next, think about the *environment* within which the influence process is taking place. Is it coercive—the kind of situation in which people need to be told what to do; where they require instruction or direction? Or is it co-operative—where mutual commitment and support are needed? Is it competitive—are there competing influences at work?

In attempting to influence a situation, the leader has to take account of the kind of relationship—or 'contract' as it's sometimes called—which exists. For example, a Sunday school superintendent who decides that he wants all his staff to arrive twenty minutes before the school is due to start so that they can have a prayer meeting, had better make sure that he understands the true nature of the contract that exists between him and them on this particular issue before deciding which method of influence to employ!

Third, there is the *effect* you want your influence attempt to have. Is it a short-term change in behaviour or a longer-term change in attitude?

Let's consider the influence methods used by the greatest leader of all time—Jesus Christ. An incident known in biblical literature as the 'Purification of the Temple' gives one insight:

When it was almost time for the Jewish Passover, Jesus went up to Jerusalem. In the temple courts he found men selling cattle, sheep and doves, and others sitting at tables exchanging money. So he made a whip of cords, and drove all from the temple area, both sheep and cattle; he scattered the coins of the money-changers and overturned their tables. To those who sold doves he said, 'Get these out of here! How dare you turn my Father's house into a market!' His disciples remembered that it is written, 'Zeal for your house will consume me' (Jn 2:13–17).

Purification of the Temple

Influence method	Power source	Environment	Desired effect
Force √	Position	Coercive √	Short-term √ (Behavioural)
Persuasion	Personality √	Co-operative	
Example	Competence		Long-term (Attitudinal)
Reward	Resources		

Jesus used force on this occasion to influence the situation and to achieve his purpose—a short-term change in behaviour! The source of his authority was a combination of physical strength and personal power. It is easy to imagine his dynamic, forceful presence.

The method was appropriate: what was needed was not a reasoned debate or an example or an incentive, but a strong directive.

Now picture this scene:

The evening meal was being served, and the devil had already prompted Judas Iscariot, son of Simon, to betray Jesus. Jesus. . . got up from the meal, took off his outer clothing, and wrapped a towel round his waist. After that, he poured water into a basin and began to wash his disciples' feet, drying them with the towel that was wrapped round him. . . When he had finished washing their feet, he put on his clothes and returned to his place. 'Do you understand what I have done for you?' he asked them. 'You call me "Teacher" and "Lord" and rightly so, for that is what I am. Now that I, your Lord and Teacher, have washed your feet, you also should wash one another's feet. I have set you an example that you should do as I have done for you' (Jn 13:2, 4–5, 12–15).

Washing the disciples' feet

Influence method	Power source	Environment	Desired effect
Force	Position	Coercive	Short-term (Behavioural)
Persuasion	Personality √	Co-operative √	
Example √	Competence		Long-term √ (Attitudinal)
Reward	Resources		

This is more than a mere demonstration; this is an influence attempt designed to have lasting impact. It illustrates the power of example as a means of influence and is a reminder that this method, in common with the others, is only as effective as the sources of power from which it stems. In this case it requires a combination of personal power—not charisma this time, but character, which is known about and can be vouched for—and position power which, in´ this instance, is not employed, but deliberately relinquished. Almost every influence attempt based on the use of example is strengthened by this latter action.

Let's think about the case of the Sunday school superintendent mentioned earlier—the one who wants to hold a short prayer meeting with his staff twenty minutes before the school commences. Assume he's decided he wants to implement this; he's not just going to put it forward as an idea to find out what the others think of it. The question remains: How is he to influence the situation and the people involved in order to get what he wants?

He could simply announce his decision, perhaps giving one or two reasons in support of it, then tell his team that he expects them all to attend, like this: 'I've got you together to tell you about something I want us to start doing as a group. I believe it will make our work among these youngsters more effective. Prayer is important, isn't it?—especially for the work we're engaged in—and so, as Superintendent, I've reached a decision.

Starting next week I want us all to meet twenty minutes before the school starts so that we can have a time of prayer. This will be good for us and for the school, so I'm asking everyone to be present.'

The choice of words could be varied, of course, but putting it this way would represent an influence attempt using force to get people to do something. Here, the influencer is mostly relying on his position to carry it off successfully.

It is worth pondering the likely outcomes of this approach:

- It may work. If the environment is generally coercive—that is, people expect to be told what to do, and provided there are no major obstacles are likely to get on and do it—then the outcome will be satisfactory.
- Whether it works will depend largely on how well the superintendent understands the situation and the people he's dealing with. It is more likely that this initiative is being launched in an environment where co-operation is required. If that is so and if there happens to be someone who feels that there is enough prayer going on already, or someone else for whom this new venture will cause a disruption of their domestic arrangements, then that co-operation will not be forthcoming, and the initiative may therefore fail.
- Presumably the effect that the superintendent wishes to create is one of long-term commitment rather than short-term compliance and this begs the question of whether taking action in this way is likely to achieve it.
- By employing this approach the superintendent is putting his positional authority, and to an extent his personal authority, on the line and it is unnecessary. He is running the risk of a confrontation in which he might come off worst and if that be the case his power base could be seriously damaged.

Another approach might be to offer some kind of incentive. This calls for a degree of lateral thinking; remember, people can be encouraged to respond positively to what is being asked of them if they perceive that in doing so their own needs are being met.

What incentives might the superintendent offer? Whatever he decides, he must be careful not to let the process degenerate into one of bribery or even negotiation.

He might try setting an example. But in doing this he will have to keep his objective clearly in view. There is little point in setting an example if others don't follow it.

Finally, he could try persuasion. In a real situation this would most likely be his first choice. However, he will probably find that the other methods of influence—force, example and reward—will invade the process, making his approach a mixture of all four.

The point is, most leaders are capable of influencing others successfully, but they do not always succeed because they do not always have sufficient appreciation of the strengths and weaknesses of their own power/influence make up and the circumstances within which it has to operate.

KEY POINTS SUMMARY

The purpose of this chapter is to explain the significance of power and influence in the leadership process; to give practical insight into how power may be acquired and used, and to highlight the ground rules for Christian leaders.

This chapter has defined influence as 'the means by which one person modifies the attitudes, behaviour and actions of others'.

Power is described as 'the capacity to exert influence'.

The key sources of the Christian leader's power have been identified and discussed:

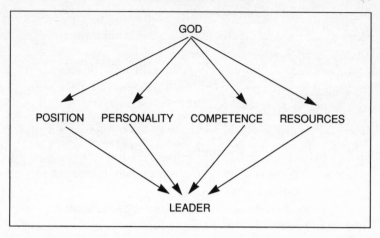

Four main methods of influence have been described:

- Force
    Physical
    Rules and procedures
- Persuasion
    Facts and logic
    Charisma/personal magnetism
- Example
    Demonstration
    Lifestyle/workstyle
- Resource
    Gift
    Negotiation (give and take)

The relationship between power and influence has been noted:

Method of influence	Power source required
	Position Power
Coercion/Force	Resource Power
	Personal Power

Persuasion	Expert Power
	Personal Power
Example	Personal Power
Reward	Resource Power
	Position Power

The implications of the foregoing have been outlined for Christian leadership. For example:

- How to choose the right influence method, taking account of:
  prevailing culture or environment;
  perceived credibility (of the leader's power source);
  desired effect (short or long term).
- What to do when the context of operation is unhelpful.
- How to acquire and develop leadership power. Ground rules for the Christian leader.
- How to guard against the negative or destructive use of power.

Each of the above has been explored in the context of the contemporary Christian scene.

GUIDE FOR ACTION

Consider the nature of your own leadership influence.

1. INFLUENCE METHODS
Consider the four methods and put a √ in the appropriate box to show the use you make of each.

	Seldom				Often
Force					
Persuasion					
Example					
Reward					

2. POWER SOURCES
Consider the four methods and put a √ in the appropriate box to show the use you make of each.

	Seldom				Often
Position					
Personal					
Expert					
Resource					

3. ENVIRONMENT

Place a √ in the appropriate box to show the frequency with which each situation occurs.

	Seldom				Often
Coercive (instruction/direction needed)					
Co-operative (agreement/support/commitment)					

4. DESIRED EFFECT

Place a √ in the appropriate box to show the frequency with which each situation occurs.

	Seldom				Often
Short-term behavioural change (quick fix)					
Longer-term attitude change (permanent shift)					

Look at the profile you have drawn. Are there any changes you'd like to make? For example, is the correlation between the influence method mostly used and the power source(s) mostly relied upon correct?

Go back over the profile and indicate any changes you'd like to make by putting a cross in the appropriate boxes.

Think about your own 'power' sources.

Do you rate your relationship with God, the ultimate source, as:

- A branch drawing its life and power from the true Vine (Jn 15:1)?
- A servant obeying his master?
- A child relying on his father?

Now think of the other four sources. How much substance does each have for you? For example, how significant is your position as a source of power? And how much credibility do others attach to your sources? For example, how do they rate your 'expert' power?

Consider each source in terms of its substance—from your

viewpoint and then its credibility in the eyes of others.

Allocate 10 points across each, first for substance and then for credibility, eg, Position—5; Personal—1; Expert—0; Resource—4.

Source	Substance	Credibility
Position		
Personal		
Expert		
Resources		

What would you like to change? Note the preferred ratings alongside those you have already established.

Think about the actions you might take to nurture and strengthen each area. For example:

Position   Do you need to become more visible?
            Are you making as much as you could of your position?
            Do you take 'ownership' of situations as often as you should?

Personal   Could you be more assertive, or less aggressive?
            Are you always as well prepared as you might be?
            Could you improve your presentation skills?
            Does your appearance let you down when it needn't?

Expert   Could you improve your knowledge and skills levels?

Resources   Make an inventory of the resources you control. Is there something you could do or give that would really count with others if it was seen to be coming from you? Are you using these resources to influence others or are you simply giving them away?

Chapter Five

THE PART PEOPLE PLAY

Wars may be fought with weapons, but they are won by men. It is the spirit of the men who follow and of the man who leads that gains the victory.

General George Patten

The eye can never say to the hand, 'I don't need you.' The head can't say to the feet, 'I don't need you.' And some of the parts that seem weakest and least important are really the most necessary (1 Cor 12:21–22, TLB).

By definition, leaders have to have followers—individuals and groups who respond positively to the leadership initiative. Much of what the leader wants to achieve depends on the co-operation and efforts of those who follow. They have been called 'the forgotten force' and all too often this is the case.

The Bible records an incident in the life of Samson, a leader whose exploits are chronicled in the Old Testament:

He went out and caught three hundred foxes and tied them tail to tail in pairs. He then fastened a torch to every pair of tails, lit the torches and let the foxes loose in the standing corn of the Philistines. He burned up the shocks and standing corn, together with the vineyards and olive groves (Judg 15:4–5).

Imagine the squealing, squirming, scratching and biting which that process must have engendered! Then afterwards the pain, and finally destruction, not only of the Philistine fields but of the foxes themselves. Good news for Samson, but bad news for the instruments of his plan—the foxes!

There are parallel circumstances which involve people instead of foxes; and leaders at all levels, however great their cause, must guard against treating their fellows as an expendable resource.

Jesus never saw men and women in that way. On one occasion a striking metaphor occurred to him:

When he saw the crowds, he had compassion on them, because they were harassed and helpless like sheep without a shepherd (Mt 9:36).

The good leader sees people not as fodder with which to feed his ego or fuel his schemes, but as individuals with unique identities who have needs and aspirations and, above all, potential to play fulfilling and crucial roles. The implications are clear, and leaders who have a genuine concern to work with their people need to do at least three things:

- Build relationships that work.
- Learn how to meet others' needs.
- Repair or renew relationships that break down.

Building relationships that work

All relationships revolve around personal needs. Have a look at this diagram:

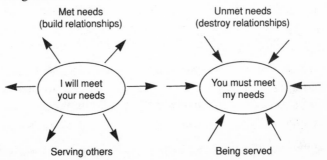

The key to building good working relationships is to bond yourself to the members of your team by showing that you are the kind of person who is committed to meeting their needs. A first step towards doing this successfully is to try and understand people rather than simply evaluate them.

Understand rather than evaluate

It's easy to evaluate others on the basis of their reputation, meeting them on their own ground so to speak, matching their words and actions with suitably chosen ones of your own in order to score points off them. This kind of thing usually leads to a battle of words and wits which no one wins.

The meeting between Jesus and the unnamed woman of Samaria, which took place in the village of Sychar beside the local well, shows the need there is to understand the other person in order to have proper dealings with them.

During the ensuing dialogue this woman recognised that she was talking to someone who saw beyond her lifestyle, who understood her at depth and who appreciated her motives and her quest for life. Her later words show her to be a woman convinced and won over to the cause of Christ.

Come, see a man who told me everything I ever did. Could this be the Christ? (Jn 4:29).

Personality is sometimes loosely defined as the sum of the differences that distinguish people. In plain language that means that everybody's different! One key to understanding people lies in being able to appreciate what these differences are. The following list, drawn up at random, illustrates the range and complexity of differences involved. People differ according to:

Age	Physique	Health
Appearance	Sex	Intelligence
Race	Religion	Politics
Education	Upbringing	Experience
Accomplishments	Beliefs	Attitudes

Abilities	Ambitions	Expectations
Temperament	Circumstances	

The list might be multiplied several times. These are typical of the things that appear in every human life and which, because of the variety of ways in which they are combined, often help to explain people's attitudes to the world around them, their actions and reactions, the decisions they take, their personal approach to solving life's problems and so on.

More significantly, from this jigsaw of personal characteristics there emerges the pattern of human needs peculiar to each individual. Over the years researchers have looked for explanations as to why people behave as they do. One in particular, Abraham Maslow, who died in 1970 having spent most of his working life as a lecturer and professor in psychology at Brandeis University in New York, developed a theory that human needs are organised on a priority or hierarchical basis. His theory starts with the assumption that every person has needs which drive him or her to act, and that these needs have different levels of importance but can be arranged in order, like this:

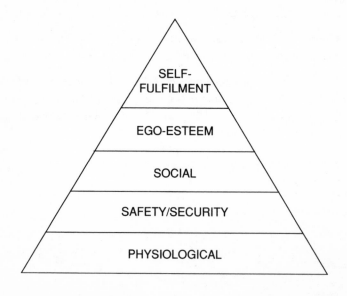

The hierarchy ranges from 'basic' needs at the bottom, through to 'higher' needs at the top. When the basic needs are satisfied, or the means are available for satisfaction, higher needs emerge and these dominate the behaviour. This is what Maslow means by human needs being organised into a 'hierarchy'.

Physiological needs

Survival, food, water, shelter, rest. These are fundamental requirements for sustaining life, and people instinctively drive in search of these first.

Safety/security needs

When the physiological needs are met, a new set of needs emerges—the need for safety and security. This translates into many forms: stability of circumstances, an ordered society, a preference for the familiar rather than the unknown, predictable outcomes, a steady job, a stable income, a home, freedom from fear.

Social needs

This is the need to belong and to feel accepted; to love and to feel loved in return. God has made us like this. The psalmist observes:

God sets the lonely in families (Ps 68:6).

As a rule, people prefer to live in groups and will seek others out that they might do so. The average person may belong to:

- a family group
- a work group
- a leisure group, club, society
- a political group
- a religious group
- an informal group.

The importance of the social need can be seen if you consider what it feels like to be shut out of a group, ignored or 'sent to Coventry'.

Ego-esteem needs

These have two dimensions—group respect and self-respect. People don't just want to belong, they want to be respected as individuals and to have some status within their group. Even the disciples of Jesus argued among themselves on one occasion about which of them should be the greatest (Lk 9:46).

The desires for reputation, recognition and appreciation stem, in part, from the need to feel wanted, important and useful. Please note that this is not a defence of such attitudes, but simply an acknowledgement that people have 'ego-esteem' needs which drive them to act in certain ways.

Jesus perceived this in his disciples and corrected their thinking on the entire issue:

Jesus, knowing their thoughts, took a little child and made him stand beside him. Then he said to them, 'Whoever welcomes this little child in my name welcomes me; and whoever welcomes me welcomes the one who sent me. For he who is least among you all—he is the greatest' (Lk 9:47–48).

Self-fulfilment needs

From a human viewpoint, this is the ultimate need. It's the feeling each person has that they should become everything they can possibly be. Words like 'growth', 'personal development' and 'achievement' help to define it.

Maslow's hierarchy has been criticised. He himself was careful to point out that it should only be taken as a guide and not as a gospel of truth. When judged in the sober light of experience his theory does go some way towards explaining why people sometimes behave as they do.

What it does not do is take into account man's essentially spiritual nature nor his quest for God. Greek philosophers, sceptical of the latter, were reminded of it in a sermon preached by the Apostle Paul which he delivered to them on Mars Hill:

From one man he made every nation of men, that they should inhabit the whole earth; and he determined the times set for them and the exact places where they should live. God did this so that men would seek him and perhaps reach out for him and find him (Acts 17:26–27).

This is further echoed in the words of Augustine, one of the early church fathers: 'O lord, thou hast made us for thyself and our hearts are restless till they find their rest in thee.'

The later writings of Maslow suggest that he sensed the weakness of a philosophy which equated self-fulfilment with the purpose of life. He had glimpsed the need to go beyond 'self-actualisation', indeed beyond the whole concept of needs, into another realm. Shortly before his death he wrote: 'I consider Humanistic, Third Force Psychology to be transitional, a preparation for a still "higher" Fourth Psychology, centred in the Cosmos rather than in human needs and interests, going beyond humanness, identity, self-actualisation and the like.' Quite what he had in mind we shall never know.

During his delivery of the Sermon on the Mount, Jesus gave some guidelines of his own. Referring to physiological and other needs he said:

Do not worry, saying, 'What shall we eat?' or, 'What shall we drink?' or, 'What shall we wear?' For the pagans run after all these things, and your heavenly Father knows that you need them. But seek first his kingdom and his righteousness, and all these things will be given to you as well (Mt 6:31–33).

These words of Jesus do not negate the notion that there are varying levels of human need which have to be met. They simply tell us that our best fulfilment comes as we find God and serve the interests of his kingdom. The principle that people are driven to act on the basis of felt needs and that they like to progress from one level of fulfilment to another is upheld; it is just a matter of how, and where best to target your efforts. Christian leaders should bear this in mind as they develop their strategies for dealing with people.

Find the need and meet it

Learning how to meet the needs of others is a second step towards successfully involving people in your leadership plans. Human behaviour doesn't always follow predictable patterns. 'Laws' which may appear to govern relationships among people often prove unreliable; there are too many imponderables.

However, there are certain guidelines which can prove helpful, providing they are seen as principles rather than hard and fast rules. As a matter of principle, people tend to want the following things—although not necessarily in this order:

- Security
- Human treatment
- Recognition
- Worthwhile work
- Opportunity for advancement
- Outlet for initiative.

Security

This can take several forms. People may feel insecure in a variety of situations and this usually happens when something of value to them appears to be under threat. Leaders should consider this carefully and be on the lookout, especially for the less obvious causes of insecurity which may be having a significant effect on the performance of individual team members.

Human treatment

'Personhood' is a word sometimes used to convey the idea that each person has worth and should be treated with dignity. Our individuality is God's choicest gift to us and should be neither scorned nor violated. People are more than a number or a cog in the machine and they expect, albeit subconsciously at times, to be treated in ways that reflect this.

Recognition

From time to time most people want, perhaps even need, some positive acknowledgement of the work they are doing. This is especially true when they feel that their performance is exceptional. Despite protestations to the contrary, if someone feels they are doing a good job they will tend to look for recognition of their efforts. This might take the form of public praise, personal thanks or some tangible reward. Leaders should appreciate that recognition by others is one of the fundamental expectations that people have; it should not be ignored.

Worthwhile work

There is a story in the Old Testament about a man who undertook a job of work and carried it out with astonishing energy and dedication:

> **When the Philistines banded together at a place where there was a field full of lentils, Israel's troops fled from them. But Shammah took his stand in the middle of the field. He defended it and struck the Philistines down, and the Lord brought about a great victory (2 Sam 23:11–12).**

To have expended so much effort and to have put himself at such risk in the process he must have felt, at the very least, that he was doing something worthwhile. People like to feel that what they are doing is worthwhile, and if they once get the idea that the work they are engaging in is the equivalent of 'digging holes and filling them in again', they will quickly lose interest and start looking for diversions!

The Christian leader, perhaps more than others, has the opportunity to engage people in worthwhile work. But occasionally he or she needs to help them see that this is the case. The Old Testament leader Nehemiah, in rebuilding the walls of the ancient city of Jerusalem, referred to his task in these words:

I am carrying on a great project and cannot go down (Neh 6:3).

Those working with him clearly felt the same way about it. Nehemiah records this in his diary:

We rebuilt the wall till all of it reached half its height, for the people worked with all their heart (Neh 4:6).

It is important for the leader and his or her followers to share the same perspective—that the work is worthwhile. If people feel that they are simply being 'used' or 'put upon' their enthusiasm will quickly evaporate.

Opportunity for advancement

Colonel John Hunt, leader of the 1953 Everest expedition which led to the conquest of the world's highest peak, was later asked at a news conference, 'Why do people climb mountains?' He replied, 'Because they are there.'

Individuals vary in terms of their personal make-up, as we have already noted, but one trait common to most is the inherent urge to accomplish, to climb higher, to be more than they are. For some this means a bigger job with greater responsibility. For others it could mean widening their sphere of influence. The readiness with which people respond when confronted with a challenging situation or when asked to fulfil a more demanding role points to the fact that, mostly, they are looking for opportunities to do and be more.

Outlet for initiative

People don't always like being told, step-by-step, what they must do and how they must do it, and many will not tolerate situations like that for long. Most prefer it when they are left to do things by themselves.

Notice the tactics of Jesus when he sent his disciples out on a mission:

After this the Lord appointed seventy-two others and sent

them two by two ahead of him to every town and place where he was about to go. He told them, 'The harvest is plentiful, but the workers are few. Ask the Lord of the harvest, therefore, to send out workers into his harvest field. Go! I am sending you out like lambs among wolves. . .' (Lk 10: 1–3).

These disciples had listened and learned and now it was their turn to act. Jesus set the task, provided some guidelines, then left them to get on with the task. His description of them as 'lambs among wolves' is a clear indication of the difficulties, even dangers, they would face. The entire situation was one in which they would be expected to use their initiative—and they did! Those same disciples came back from their mission with glowing reports of success. Their enthusiasm was unrestrained, if a little misguided:

The seventy-two returned with joy and said, 'Lord, even the demons submit to us in your name.' He replied, '. . .do not rejoice that the spirits submit to you, but rejoice that your names are written in heaven' (Lk 10:17, 20)

Foundations for good relations

When your behaviour as a leader matches the needs or expectations of your followers, you will begin to create a climate in which good, productive relations can flourish. This is not as complicated as it sounds. There is a strategy you can employ that will achieve results. It requires you to carry out four basic actions. If you make a practice of these consistently, over a period of time you will find yourself fulfilling the major expectations of those around, almost as a matter of course. The following diagram illustrates this:

Leader's behaviour	Followers' expectations
Give credit when due	→ Human treatment → Recognition → Security
Let each person know how they are progressing	→ Security → Recognition
Tell people in advance about changes that will affect them	→ Human treatment → Security
Make the best use of each person's ability	→ Opportunity for advancement → Worthwhile work → Outlet for initiative

Give credit when due

This pays dividends, but it's worth taking time to think through the best ways of doing it. There's no need to go over the top. A simple 'thank-you' for a job well done, along with a few well-chosen words which show that you've understood the amount of effort put in or the complexity of the task undertaken, is often enough. Don't overdo it—you'll run the risk of being branded insincere or a flatterer. Do it too often and the impact will be lost.

Look for circumstances where someone's efforts have been outstanding or their contribution particularly helpful. Where credit is due, give it in ways that are meaningful. Avoid the use of bland, throw-away comments like, 'Well done, man! That was brilliant!' and try not to adopt a casual, off-hand manner of delivery.

Giving credit where due has a reassuring effect on those who receive it. The need to feel secure is satisfied. It will be construed as human treatment, and clearly it also counts as recognition.

Let each person know how they are progressing

People need feedback; without it they won't know whether they are moving in the right direction or at the right speed. Feedback on lack of progress is also important. Confronting people with the realities of their situation concentrates their minds on what has to be done if success is to be realised.

Additionally, people *want* to finish what they are doing. The more significant the task, the stronger the need to complete it. John Wesley called this 'the lust to finish'. It is a sound principle. If people know that they are moving forward, it leads them to increase their efforts.

When you are in the habit of letting people know how they are getting along, they will interpret this as human treatment. They may even see it as a form of recognition. When people are uncertain about how they are doing, it makes them feel insecure. Giving them positive feedback in this way allays any unnecessary fears.

Tell people in advance about changes that will affect them

The words of Jesus, spoken in the Upper Room on the eve of his crucifixion, are deeply poignant:

> **All this I have spoken while still with you. But the Counsellor, the Holy Spirit, whom the Father will send in my name, will teach you all things and will remind you of everything I have said to you. Peace I leave with you; my peace I give you. I do not give to you as the world gives. Do not let your hearts be troubled and do not be afraid. You heard me say, 'I am going away and I am coming back to you.' If you loved me, you would be glad that I am going to the Father, for the Father is greater than I. I have told you now before it happens, so that when it does happen you will believe (Jn 14:25–29).**

Whether the news is good or bad, people generally like to hear it in advance so that they can have time to adjust to the changes that are forthcoming. This has a direct bearing on the need for security; people have a remarkable capacity for coming to terms with things once they know about them. But uncertainty is like a creeping paralysis, immobilising the will and the actions.

Make the best use of each person's ability

Individuals have differing gifts and strengths:

> **Some of us have been given special ability as apostles; to others he has given the gift of being able to preach well; some have special ability in winning people to Christ, helping them to trust him as their Savior; still others have a gift for caring for God's people as a shepherd does his sheep, leading and teaching them in the ways of God. Why is it that he gives us these special abilities to do certain things best? It is that God's people will be equipped to do better work for him, building up the church, the body of Christ, to a position of strength and maturity (Eph 4:11–12, TLB).**

Each person has his own unique set of gifts, skills, creative talents and weaknesses. Unfortunately, many leaders think that their chief aim should be to try and eliminate, or at least greatly reduce, those areas of weakness in their followers. But this can turn out to be counter-productive. By spending considerable amounts of time, effort and even money in coaching and training, a leader can help others in the areas of their greatest shortcomings, but excessive time and effort spent trying to eliminate weaknesses may also lead to a reduction in the personal strengths of the individual.

The rule is, 'Play to your strengths, not your weaknesses.' Of course, this doesn't mean that weak areas are to be ignored, but the tactic should be to curb them, not convert them into strengths. Leaders who are concerned to use people's gifts, skills and creativity to advantage should arrange for them to work in situations that make the most use of their particular strengths, and avoid putting them into those that will expose their weaknesses by requiring them to do things they are never likely to be much good at.

Serious attempts to make the best use of each person's abilities by placing them in situations where they are best suited or which provide opportunities for further development of their skills, will serve to meet their need for worthwhile work, give them an outlet for initiative and provide them with opportunities for advancement.

Repairing relationships when they break down

There are four main categories of relationship:

- Co-operation
- Retaliation
- Domination
- Isolation

You can recognise each by the following characteristics:

Co-operation

Mutual commitment to meet the other person's need.

- Mutual trust and respect.
- Mutual use of gifts, skills and creativity.
- Joint development of solutions to problems.
- Productive relationships.
- Personal commitment to the relationships.
- Continued strengthening of relationships.

Retaliation

Attempts to make others conform to what you want.

- Aggressive attitudes towards others.
- Attitudes that view others as objects in your way.
- Struggle for domination.
- Continual conflict.
- An eventual winner and loser.

Domination

'Loser' controlled by a 'winner'.

- Loser's personality suffocated.
- Mutual loss of respect.
- Loser's creativity and skills not used.
- Loser resorts to manipulation.
- Loser eventually concludes situation is hopeless and stops trying to get needs met.

Isolation

Other person mentally 'blocked out'.

- Communication stopped
- Mutual distrust
- Problems unsolved
- Needs unmet
- Mutual unconcern
- Productivity decreases
- Relationship terminates

The cycle of deterioration within a relationship is clearly marked by these four stages. They represent a downward spiral of progressively worsening conditions and increasingly dreadful prospects.

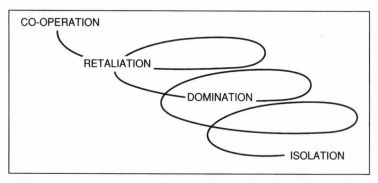

Relationship breakdown is something which leaders must detect at an early stage and deal with promptly. The longer the process is allowed to continue, the more difficult it becomes to rectify.

Three simple steps suggest themselves for consideration:

- Detect the problem.
- Define the problem.
- Deal with the problem.

Detecting the problem

How do you know when you've got a problem?

Every situation sends out signals which allow its condition to be monitored. Problem situations involving a deterioration of personal and group relationships are no different.

In those days when the number of disciples was increasing, the Grecian Jews among them complained against the Hebraic Jews because their widows were being overlooked in the daily distribution of food (Acts 6:1).

Relationships in the early church at Jerusalem were breaking down; the first tell-tale sign was a complaint. Soon the spirit of co-operation which was proving so fruitful would give way to one of retaliation. If this continued unchecked it would give place to one of domination, and ultimately this would lead to isolation of members one from the other.

Be on the alert for signs of breakdown. Generally there are three ways in which a problem may be detected:

- Complaints
- Observation
- Deteriorating 'performance'

Leaders ought to be continually monitoring the status of relationships within their group, church or organisation and be ready to act promptly, as did the first church leaders:

So the Twelve gathered all the disciples together and said, 'It would not be right for us to neglect the ministry of the word of God in order to wait on tables. . .' (Acts 6:2).

This introduces the second step in repairing relationships that have broken down, namely, defining the problem.

Defining the problem

This diagram illustrates the way in which a problem may be defined:

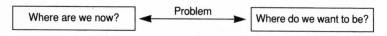

Think of the problem as being the gap between how you would like things to be and how they are at present. The solution lies in finding a way of bridging this gap. So, when faced with a human relations problem the first thing to do is define the situation precisely as you would like it to be. Next, define it as it stands at present.

You will need to make use of facts to do both these things. Resist the temptation to jump to conclusions at this stage, even though a solution may appear to be showing itself. Concentrate on 'what' rather than 'why' and 'how'.

There are many sources of information; gather it wherever you can. Some will come from your own knowledge of the circumstances. You may have to check on certain facts to ensure their accuracy or that your understanding of them is correct.

Another source is people; talk to them, ask questions of them and be prepared to listen. You can separate fact from opinion later. Reviewing the record is another way of finding out facts. Everything has a history and in many instances there will be a record you can consult. This may be written or it may be a matter of custom and practice. Don't ignore any of it; refer to it.

This process takes time. The outcome of the apostles' deliberations is summed up in a few sentences in Acts 6, but this does not imply that they arrived at the solution to their problem in as many minutes!

Spend time on the definition process; it pays dividends. Remember: a problem well defined is a problem half-solved.

Dealing with the problem

Dealing with the problem has four phases.

1. Analyse the root cause. Now is the time to ask 'why' questions. The symptoms which enabled you to detect the problem will most likely represent the tip of an iceberg. Invariably there is more to human problems than meets the eye at first. Look for possible causes, then narrow these down until you have a list of most likely causes.

2. Develop potential solutions. The aim should be to generate a range of possible solutions which address the root cause, then close down on the one which is best. Sometimes the process of turning up the right solution defies analysis. Solving the problem described in Acts 6 led to the appointment of the first church deacons.

Brothers, choose seven men from among you who are known to be full of the Spirit and wisdom. We will turn this responsibility over to them and will give our attention to prayer and the ministry of the word (Acts 6:3–4).

Logic and common sense have their part to play, but so do prayer and the influence of the word of God and the creative insight that is given by the Holy Spirit. This was a case without precedent and the corresponding solution was novel.

However, to assist the process of deciding which is the best or most appropriate solution, it is sometimes helpful to have a set of criteria in mind which will allow you to think about potential solutions in rational ways and to make sound judgements. Here are some possible contenders for your list:

• Biblical principles involved
• Timescale
• Cost
• Resources needed
• Ease of implementation
• Within your control

Now you can decide on what to do. Comparing each possible solution against the criteria you have set will help you to settle on a preferred option. You can, if you wish, make use of a simple solution matrix.

Potential solutions	Criteria					Totals
	1	2	3	4	5	
A						
B						
C						
D						

The rating might be done on a simple YES/NO basis, or for more complex issues on a HIGH/MEDIUM/LOW basis or even a score out of ten. Whatever you decide to do, don't treat the rating process as a 'sausage machine' type of approach. See it instead as a means of promoting a more rational thought process designed to prompt discussion and remove emotional or 'pet' solutions.

3. Implementing the solution

This proposal pleased the whole group. They chose Stephen, a man full of faith and of the Holy Spirit; also Philip, Procorus, Nicanor, Timon, Parmenas, and Nicolas from Antioch, a convert to Judaism. They presented these men to the apostles, who prayed and laid their hands on them (Acts 6:5).

Having decided what to do, the next step is to implement the solution. Plan it carefully; think about the timing of your actions—the right solution introduced at the wrong time can have disastrous results.

Consider also whether you need to consult anyone before implementing any new arrangements. Are there any procedures to be gone through?

Are you planning to introduce the solution personally, or will that be someone else's job? Will you need any help with the implementation programme? If so, who will provide it?

4. *Monitor progress and check on the results.* You need to ensure that the solution you have chosen to introduce is fully implemented. More importantly, you need to follow up your actions to check that the solution is working. How will you do this? If you need to make any changes, how will you make them?

So the word of God spread. The number of disciples in Jerusalem increased rapidly, and a large number of priests became obedient to the faith (Acts 6:7).

Relationships restored; problem solved!

KEY POINTS SUMMARY

All relationships are formed on the basis of needs.

Met needs build relationships; unmet needs destroy relationships. People need:

- Security
- Human treatment
- Recognition
- Worthwhile work
- Opportunity for advancement
- Outlet for initiative

Four rules for building good relationships described:

- Give credit where due.
- Let people know how they are progressing.
- Tell people in advance about changes that will affect them.
- Make the best use of each person's ability.

Four types of relationship defined:

- Co-operation
- Retaliation

- Domination
- Isolation

The steps to repairing relationships that break down or are deteriorating discussed:

- Detecting problems
- Defining problems
- Dealing with problems

GUIDE FOR ACTION

Do you need to work at establishing good relations within your group?

Assess the significance of the four rules. Can you make use of any or all to create the right kind of working relationships?

Determine the current status of relationships within your group in terms of:

- Co-operation
- Retaliation
- Domination
- Isolation

Have you a problem? Develop an action plan for resolving it.

Chapter Six

STYLES AND CONTEXT

*You do not lead by hitting people over the head; that's assault, not
leadership.*

Anonymous

*Feed the flock of God; care for it willingly. . .Don't be tyrants, but
lead them by your good example* (1 Pet 5:2–3, TLB).

*Leaders are great believers in circumstances. If they don't like the
circumstances they change them.*

Anonymous

The process of leadership involves:

- The use of *power and influence*—the capacity to affect the
  behaviour of others.
- Creating and maintaining the right kind of *relationships with
  people*—harnessing their talents and skills.
- Employing a *style* of leadership which suits the *context of
  operations*.

So far we have dealt with the first two. This chapter explains
what leadership style is and shows the importance of employing
the right style in given situations.

What is leadership style?

Leadership style simply refers to the way in which leaders lead.
It is about how you, as a leader, are trying to bring your influence

to bear upon those around you in order to achieve your goals. Your leadership style governs your approach in particular situations and to a certain extent reflects your attitude towards the people with whom you are working.

It is possible to identify four distinct leadership styles:

Autocratic

Here the leader takes decisions alone and expects his followers to carry them out without question. Effectively, the style is one of 'telling'—followers seldom have any direct say in the decision-making process. Many people try to adopt this style. They think it is expected of them as leaders.

Saul, Israel's first king, provides an interesting case study of an autocratic leader in action. He was extremely decisive and used his position to drive people into following him in battle (1 Sam 11). But he overstepped his authority by performing priestly sacrifices (chapter 13). Later, his quick decisions and pride almost caused the death of his son Jonathan (chapter 14).

Saul was happy to accept the help of a comparatively unknown youth when it was to his advantage (chapter 17), but generally his style was autocratic and he was unwilling to share his power and position with anyone (chapters 18–27).

Autocratic leadership is not always bad. There are situations in which it is quite appropriate, even essential, for example:

- In emergencies, where time taken to make decisions is more critical than the quality of the decision itself or the commitment of subordinates.
- When people are unfamiliar with the detail of their jobs.
- When severe disciplinary action is needed.

Persuasive

The leader still takes the decisions alone, but because he believes that people are better motivated if they feel that the decision is the right one, he spends time persuading them that this is so.

Here, the leader makes the decision and then 'sells' it to everyone by giving sensible reasons, stressing key advantages and so on.

This kind of approach is appropriate in situations where the leader alone is in full possession of all information needed to make the decision, but where a high degree of commitment is also required from others.

Autocrats and persuaders:

- Seldom let others make decisions, and often consider their views to be the most valid.
- Frequently lack confidence in other people's abilities.
- Usually apply other people's ideas only if they agree with them.
- Are often action-orientated.

Consultative

This kind of leader confers with his group before taking decisions and will readily take the group's feelings into account when making decisions.

Generally the consultative leader presents ideas, invites questions and suggestions, then decides.

This approach is appropriate when:

- Information needed to make decisions is distributed among group members.
- Creative problem solving is needed.

Reference has already been made in an earlier chapter to the incident described in Acts 6:1–7. This is a good example of the consultative style of leadership in action. As the church grew, some people's needs were no longer being met—a problem growing churches often face today.

The record of this incident implies that several principles were at work and these demonstrate the consultative leadership style:

- The leaders got the people with the problem to work on the solution.
- The leaders reserved the right to review the proposals and make the final decision.

- The leaders were able to work on other important projects while the solution to this particular problem was being implemented.

Consultative leaders:

- Ask for contributions from other members of their team on a regular basis.
- Never make decisions without getting the input of those likely to be affected by them.
- Are willing to delegate some decision-making responsibilities to others but retain the power of veto.
- Usually try to weigh all suggested alternatives before making a decision.

Participative

The leader puts issues to his subordinates and allows the decision to emerge from within the group. In using this participative style, the leader hands over the power of deciding to the group, having spelled out the choices which must be made and having defined the boundaries or limits which the decision must respect.

This approach is appropriate in situations similar to those which make a consultative approach suitable, but where a high degree of commitment and enthusiasm is essential. It is also suited to circumstances in which people are competent in performing their tasks and where it may be necessary to keep highly qualified or experienced people motivated.

When the participative style of leadership is in operation the leader:

- Becomes a team member, like the others.
- Frequently accepts the team's ideas, even when they differ from his own.
- Focuses on stimulating creativity and innovation within the team, becoming, for all practical purposes, a facilitator or catalyst.

What kind of leader are you?

At this stage it will be helpful for you to try and determine what your preferred leadership style is—that is, the approach you lean towards and which you are most likely to use.

People go about their work in different ways. Some enjoy work which requires precision and order; others like the kind of situation which lets them exercise their creativity and ideas. There is evidence which suggests that work preferences influence not only the way in which people go about their tasks, but also the way in which they are likely to behave if they find themselves in situations which require them to exercise leadership.

Do you know what your basic work preferences are? Completing the following questionnaire will give you some insight into these and at the same time, an idea of your preferred leadership style.

Allocate a number from the scale below which best corresponds with your own preference and insert in the box provided:

0	1	2	3
Does not describe my preferred approach at all	Describes my preferred approach a little	Describes my approach a fair amount of the time	Describes my preferred approach most of the time

I like to work:

	Column C	Column E
Systematically	☐	
Creatively		☐
With hard facts	☐	
Inventing/designing		☐
Building/producing	☐	

	C	E
Theorising		☐
Using imagination		☐
In an orderly way	☐	
Planning	☐	
Exploring possibilities		☐
Spontaneous action		☐
Searching and changing		☐
Consolidating	☐	
Taking risks		☐
Using insight		☐
Being practical	☐	
Using intuition		☐
Rationally	☐	
Methodically	☐	
With change and newness		☐
With standards and systems	☐	
With real things	☐	
TOTAL	═══	═══

The 'C' column stands for the *controlling* approach. A high score here shows that you like to work with facts and to plan carefully. You prefer working to rules and guidelines where these exist. People with a high 'C' score often have high standards for the work they do and they expect others to keep to them. Sometimes this leads to a decisive, judgemental style; at other times it may result in a supportive, helping approach to establishing order.

The 'E' column represents the *exploring* approach. A high 'E' score shows that you like to gather information in an innovative but not particularly systematic way. The 'E' approach is more spontaneous, more intuitive, more open than the methodical approach. A high 'E' score shows that you like to use your imagination, consider a range of possibilities, theorise, search for new ways of doing things. The person with a high 'E' score is likely to have leaps of insight which go beyond facts immediately available.

Controlling can be equated with restrictive forms of leadership which tend to impose and prescribe. Exploring is linked to permissive leadership which allows for flexibility and consultation and leaves room for participation.

Those with a bias towards the control end of the spectrum will tend to operate in the autocratic or persuasive mode. Those who lean towards the explorer side will tend to lead using a consultative and at times a participative style.

This should not be taken to imply that autocrats and persuaders are vigorous, dynamic, decisive types, while those who favour a more participative or consultative style are somehow vacillating and 'wimpish'. Each of the four styles is perfectly viable in its own right as a method of exercising leadership, but it may not always be the most appropriate in a given situation.

How to select the most appropriate leadership style

A carpenter working with wood or a sculptor with stone both know that the materials they employ possess unique properties. Texture, finish, depth of colour, grain direction and other factors peculiar to a particular piece all have to be taken into account if proper use is to be made of it. The craftsman knows that he must work *with* the material and not against it if he wants to bring out the best in it. So it is with the leader, striving to achieve his objectives. He must be aware of the facets of his situation and try to work with them rather than drive hard against them.

He must take account of the people around him, of their preferences and of how they are organised. He has to appreciate the nature of the task, of how it is structured and of how it can best be executed. Above all, he must remember that he is not working in a vacuum; all his activities take place within a certain context which will allow him to do some things and prevent him from doing others.

The leader who is able to co-operate with the conditions he faces will find that his creative purpose is enhanced; the result of his endeavours will be better than planned.

The point to note about leadership styles is that there is no single style which is always right or always best. Christ used various leadership styles in the course of his ministry. When driving the money-changers out of the Temple his approach was autocratic (Jn 2:13–16). On other occasions he gave his disciples authority to perform many of the tasks he had himself been doing, making them part of his team (Mt 10:1–15).

The leader's concern must always be to employ, as far as he is able, the kind of style which suits the situation he is facing. In trying to determine this, there are four factors to take into consideration:

- The leader and his preferred leadership style.
- The 'led' and their preferred leadership style.
- The task/mission; its nature, importance and timescale.
- The environment or organisational context within which leader and led operate.

Leadership will be at its most effective when the preferences of the leader and his or her followers and the requirements of the job all fit together.

Imagine a situation in which there is a leader whose style is to control. He is working with a group of people who like to have some freedom over how they do things and they are working on a task which is loosely defined with no tight timescales to worry about.

The diagram which follows shows this:

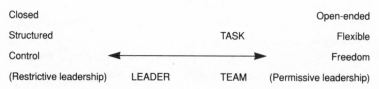

Closed			Open-ended
Structured		TASK	Flexible
Control	← →		Freedom
(Restrictive leadership)	LEADER	TEAM	(Permissive leadership)

Here, the task and the subordinates 'fit', but the leader is out on a limb. Can you picture any real-life situation which might be depicted by this diagram? A bishop overseeing the work of his diocese perhaps? Or a senior church leader co-ordinating the activities of a number of house-group leaders?

Whatever the circumstances, these three factors must coincide or at least come fairly close together, otherwise things simply will not work well. If they remain too far apart the group will stop functioning as a group, the quality of the end product will suffer, or the job will not get done at all.

Take, for example, the job of flower arranging. Let's suppose, as is the case in many churches, that the responsibility for this rests with a small group of ladies whose task is to decorate the interior of the church with fresh flowers each week in a tasteful and pleasing way. Their responsibility also includes decorating the church on special occasions in ways that reflect the nature of that occasion, for example, Harvest Festival days, Easter Sundays, weddings and so on.

This is a creative task, difficult to define, and is best carried out by people who are knowledgeable and experienced in this kind of work. People like this will, naturally, want plenty of control over their work and provided the end results are satisfactory it's reasonable to let them get on with it.

In these circumstances it is clear that the leader's approach should be flexible and supportive with minimum direction and little direct involvement. Suppose a leader comes on the scene whose style is different. He still wants to have little direct involvement in the doing of the work but his approach is autocratic. He does the group's thinking for them and tells them precisely what he wants them to do. He specifies the number of flower arrangements needed and where they are to be positioned. He even says what kind of flowers he wants in each vase!

Can you imagine the likely outcome? This group will not appreciate the kind of leadership which reduces them to functionaries, automatons whose task is simply to get flowers, put them in vases and place them in certain positions around the church! Also, the task is not the sort which lends itself to being tackled in this prescriptive way.

In the above scenario a powerful leader will often succeed in pulling the team and the task towards his way of working, but in the process of doing so he runs the risk of damaging relationships between himself and his subordinates which in turn can have serious long-term effects on the partnership.

On the other hand, he could try moving towards them by adjusting his leadership style to one which is more consultative or even participative. This is easier said than done, however. The idea that leaders can switch from one style to another at will is false, but it is worth making the effort because it represents a better short-term strategy.

The foregoing illustrates the complexity of the leadership situation, and this complexity is further compounded by a fourth factor—the organisational context or setting in which it is taking place. The leader, his team of followers and the task they are engaged in, don't operate in a vacuum. Changing his own style, the group's leadership preferences and the ways in which its work is structured so that all three accommodate each other are best tackled over a longer period of time, but the context of operations will have a big bearing on the extent to which the leader is able to do this.

Here is a simple model which will help you assess how appropriate your style is in your present circumstances and also lead you to see the kind of changes you may need to make in order to bring about a more effective leadership situation.

Think first about the leader's position on the 'structured to flexible' scale. Five factors will influence this. Consider each in turn and circle a number that represents your view of yourself.

THE LEADER

I don't think my sub-ordinates should be involved in planning, deciding, controlling.	1 2 3 4 5	I think my subordinates should be involved in planning, deciding, con-trolling.

My habitual style of leading is autocratic.	1 2 3 4 5	My habitual style of leading is participative.
I prefer not to give people too much control over their work.	1 2 3 4 5	I have confidence in my people and trust them to achieve the necessary results in doing their work.
I like to be able to predict outcomes and to minimise risks.	1 2 3 4 5	I am happy to relinquish control of situations.
I feel that my contribution to my group's work is vital.	1 2 3 4 5	I don't think my contribution to the work of my group is critical.

Add together the numbers you circled and divide by 5.

A score of between 1.0 and 2.5 shows you have a marked preference for structure and control and that your approach is likely to be restrictive.

A score between 2.5 and 5.0 shows a preference for flexibility and freedom and a permissive style of leading.

The factors which influence where you as a leader find yourself on the scale will often be in conflict, but the net result will be to place you somewhere on the scale between 'structured' and 'flexible'. Note this and consider next your team of followers.

Their preference for a particular style of leadership will be influenced by another five factors. Think of these in turn and circle a number which you feel reflects their view. (Why not let your subordinates complete this as well? You might find the results most enlightening!)

THE SUBORDINATES

My subordinates don't feel confident in themselves and feel the need for guidance and control.	1 2 3 4 5	My subordinates have a high estimate of their competence and want control of their work.
My group like things to be done in a clear, step-by-step, orderly way.	1 2 3 4 5	My group like ambiguity and freedom to alter things as they go along.
My group have a low view of the importance of this task and lack interest in it.	1 2 3 4 5	My group are keenly interested in this task and view it as important.
My group are not used to working together and have little past experience.	1 2 3 4 5	My group are used to working together and members have respect for each other's ability.
Members of my group are older and are used to being told what to do.	1 2 3 4 5	Members of my group are young, well educated and 'raring to go'.

Add together the numbers you circled and divide by 5.

A score of between 1.0 and 2.5 shows that the group have a marked preference for a structured approach and will respond to a leadership style which controls and directs them in their work.

A score between 2.5 and 5.0 shows a preference for flexibility and freedom and for a permissive style of leadership. Note this and compare it with your preferred leadership style.

Now consider the task you are engaged in. Whether this needs to be structured or is best left open-ended will depend on four factors. Consider each in turn and circle the number you feel best describes it.

THE TASK

The task is routine, requires obedience and implementation.	1 2 3 4 5	The task requires initiative, involves problem solving and a certain amount of 'pioneering' skill.
The timescale of this task is short.	1 2 3 4 5	The timescale of this task is long.
The task is complicated from an organisational standpoint.	1 2 3 4 5	The task is complex and technically difficult.
The task is routine in nature.	1 2 3 4 5	The task is important—much is at stake.

Add together the numbers you circled and divide by 4.

A score of between 1.0 and 1.5 indicates that the task needs to be carefully programmed and that a structured approach is preferable.

A score between 2.5 and 4.0 reveals a need for flexibility.

Compare the positions of *leader, subordinate* and *task*, and note the degree of 'fit' or 'misfit'. Confronted with a lack of fit you must decide on the kind of adjustments you need to make. It is easiest to alter your own style, but you shouldn't blind yourself to the long-term benefits that might be gained if instead you were to redefine or redesign the task or develop the group so that its preferences changed.

In thinking about whether to adapt to the situation or pull it towards you, it is interesting to consider what might happen when the leadership is predominantly male or predominantly female.

Some research shows that men are less inclined to change their basic style than women, and when they do, the attempt is likely to be more clumsy.

Where the decision is one of pulling the situation in to suit the leader, the tactics that women may instinctively adopt are markedly different from those employed by men, and are likely to be much less direct.

As to the question of which brand of leadership is most likely to succeed in a given situation, it is of course impossible to say. But male versus female leadership remains a significant and intriguing factor.

A fourth component which must be taken into account is the context in which your leadership efforts are taking place. A leader is never completely free to behave as he would want. The organisation to which he belongs will constrain him. There are norms, practices, traditions and expectations of behaviour which will hinder his attempts to alter what is going on around him. For example, a bishop is not free to move his manpower around as he would like. Some sections of the Christian church have strong central government which can limit the powers of a local minister. The manager of a Christian bookshop which is part of a chain of shops will be constrained by policy and procedural considerations within which he or she has to work.

The key question is: How much freedom does the context allow the leader to have to alter his or her personal style? To try and change the group? To restructure the way the task is done? Context doesn't just mean the organisation with its traditions and its taboos and its power structure. It includes things like the variety of tasks which are being undertaken; few are carried out in isolation. Then there is the variety of subordinates involved. This too can complicate the leadership environment and limit the capacity to act.

Finally, there is the power position of the leader within the organisation, and the nature of his or her relationship to the group—both of which have been discussed in earlier chapters. These must be taken into account and can be factors which either limit the freedom of the leader or give him or her greater licence.

In a word, leaders, especially Christian leaders, can never have a licence to do as they please. Apart from some obvious spiritual principles at stake, several quite earthy constraints are at work too. Therefore a leader's style and the context in which he or she has to operate are highly significant in determining leadership effectiveness.

Modifying your style

If style is simply a matter of personality, then little can be done to alter it. It takes more than a few role-playing exercises to turn, say, a brusque, reserved fifty-year-old into a charismatic, glad-handing, back-slapping extrovert!

But if we think of style as behaviour which can be modified to suit different circumstances, we are on firmer ground. There is a useful framework for understanding this. Think of the leader's behaviour as either giving direction or providing support. Leaders can use these two types of behaviour in varying amounts. For example, the level of direction can range from giving someone—or a whole group—complete autonomy for a particular task, to issuing detailed orders. Support can vary from a low-level involvement with the group or individual to continuous, active encouragement.

We can picture it like this:

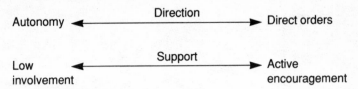

Directive behaviour includes:

- Setting objectives for others.
- Deciding how things should be done and giving orders to those doing it.
- Organising resources needed for a particular piece of work.
- Setting deadlines.
- Stipulating particular ways of working.

- Checking to make sure things get done to the right standard.

Supportive behaviour includes:

- Seeking suggestions and ideas about the way work should be done.
- Encouraging people to solve their problems as a group rather than simply imposing solutions.
- Providing encouragement and praise and being open about information.
- Listening to what others have to say and making an effort to take account of their views.
- Communicating.

The question to ask is: How much direction and how much support does the group or individual need in any given situation?

- High direction/low support calls for *instruction*.
- High direction/high support calls for a *coaching* style.
- Low direction/high support calls for *encouragement*.
- Low direction/low support signals that *delegation* is appropriate.

This can be shown diagrammatically, thus:

Four Styles of Leadership Behaviour

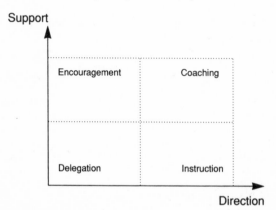

To illustrate this, here are four typical leadership situations. Study each one, then try to decide what kind of behaviour is most appropriate for the leader to adopt.

Situation 1

You are considering a change. Your followers have a fine record of accomplishment. They respect the need for change. Should you:

1. Allow group involvement in developing the change, but not be too directive?
2. Announce the change and implement with close supervision?
3. Allow the group to formulate its own direction?
4. Incorporate the group's recommendations, but you direct the change?

Situation 2

Members of your team are unable to solve a particular problem. You have normally left them alone. Group performance and interpersonal relations are good. Should you:

1. Work with the group and together engage in problem solving?
2. Let the group work it out themselves?
3. Act quickly and firmly to correct and redirect?
4. Encourage the group to work on the problem and be supportive of their efforts?

Situation 3

You stepped into an efficiently-run Christian organisation. The previous incumbent controlled the situation tightly. You want to maintain a productive situation, but you would like to start humanising the environment. Should you:

1. Do what you can to make people feel important and involved?
2. Emphasise the importance of deadlines and tasks?
3. Intentionally not intervene?
4. Get the group involved in decision making, but see that deadlines are met?

Situation 4

The performance of your group has been deteriorating during the last few months. Members have been unconcerned with meeting objectives. They have continually needed reminding to have their tasks done on time. Redefining roles and responsibilities has helped in the past. Should you:

1. Allow the group to formulate its own direction?
2. Incorporate group recommendations, but see that deadlines are met?
3. Redefine roles and responsibilities and supervise carefully?
4. Allow group involvement in determining roles and responsibilities, but not be too directive?

Situation 1 suggests a low need for direction and a need for support. Let the group decide the best way to bring about the change you want. Delegate (Action 3).

Situation 2 suggests a low need for direction, but a high need for support. Encourage them (Action 4).

Situation 3. A coaching style is needed here; high support and high direction (Action 4).

Situation 4 calls for high direction and low support. Instruction is needed (Action 3).

You may disagree with some of these analyses, but the value of this approach lies in the fact that it conditions you to consider situations in a fairly structured way and this can be helpful in determining the kind of behaviour which is appropriate.

KEY POINTS SUMMARY

Four distinct leadership styles can be identified:

- Autocratic
- Persuasive
- Consultative
- Participative

There is no single style which is always right or always best.

There are four factors to be taken into account when establishing the most appropriate leadership style:

- The leader and his preferred leadership style.
- The 'led' and their preferred leadership style.
- The task/mission; its nature, importance and timescale.
- The environment or organisational context within which leader and led operate.

You can modify your style by adopting a combination of directive and supportive behaviours. This will lead you to either:

- Encourage
- Instruct
- Coach
- Delegate

GUIDE FOR ACTION

Use the model to assess your current leadership situation. Are you employing an appropriate leadership style?

Are there any other changes you think you might make—to the team or to the task?

PART THREE

Leading with Vision

Leaders articulate and define what has previously remained implicit and unsaid; then they invent images, metaphors and models that provide a focus for new attention. By so doing they consolidate or challenge the prevailing wisdom. . . They concern themselves with their organisations' basic purposes and general direction. They are not 'incrementalists', they create new ideas, new policies, new methodologies. They change the basic metabolism of their organisations. They 'create dangerously' instead of simply mastering basic routines. Their visions and intentions are compelling, pulling people towards them. Intensity coupled with commitment is magnetic. And these intense personalities do not have to coerce people to pay attention; they are so intent on what they are doing that, like a child completely absorbed with creating a sand castle in a sand box, they draw others in.

Leaders, *Bennis and Nanus*

Chapter Seven

VISION: SEEING BEYOND CURRENT REALITIES

The task of the leader is to get his people from where they are to where they have not been. The public does not understand the world into which it is going. Leaders must invoke the alchemy of great vision. Those leaders who do not are ultimately judged failures, even though they may be popular at the moment!

Henry Kissenger

Leaders need vision. Whether you are a bishop, bookshop owner, youth pastor or prayer group co-ordinator makes little difference. If you are to exercise true leadership, you must begin by having a clear view of where you want to take your organisation or the part of it for which you are responsible. You must be clear about what you want it to become and about what you want to achieve with your followers. This 'picture of a preferred future' is essential—it is more than just managing day-to-day activities with improved efficiency or making arrangements so that things run more smoothly.

Where there is no vision the people perish, (Prov 29:18, AV).

The pages of history recount the deeds of people whose lives were directed by a strong sense of purpose. Most of the major achievements on record are attributable to men and women with powerful dreams.

Moses, the man of God, foresaw a land of promise flowing with plenty, towards which he was leading God's people. This vision became the focus of his actions. Nehemiah, a Jewish exile who rose to occupy an important place in the administration of a foreign king, had vision. He pictured the ancient city of Jerusalem with its ruined walls rebuilt and the life of its community restored. This inspired him to act and to compel others to act with him.

Martin Luther King, leader of the black peoples of America, active in the struggle for justice and equality, had a vision. He voiced it on numerous occasions, the most memorable of which was during a speech he gave in Memphis, Tennessee on 3rd April 1968, the day before his assassination:

> I have a dream. I've been to the mountain top. And I've looked over and I've seen the promised land. I may not get there with you, but I want you to know that we as a people will get to the promised land. So I'm happy tonight. I'm not worried about anything. I'm not fearing any man. Mine eyes have seen the glory of the company of the Lord.

Conversely when things like vision, purpose and ideals crumble or are cast aside, the enterprise ends up by going through the motions and eventually becomes just a tired bureaucracy with no purpose other than to preserve its own existence. Vision energises the leader. It determines his or her objectives and influences the way in which the followers are led.

Leaders project images, invent metaphors and provide models which become the focus for new attention. A common quality of leaders in every age has been this ability to select, develop and articulate an appropriate vision of the future. This chapter deals with what vision is, how it is acquired and how it is developed to the stage where it has meaning and substance and can be shared with others.

Pictures of what the future looks like usually exist already at individual and organisational level. When they are weak, uncertain, negative or conflicting, fear and resistance and apathy are often present too. Rallying people towards a compelling picture of the preferred future is an important first step for any leader.

Vision gives birth to goals and strategies for achieving those goals; it gives meaning and purpose to people's efforts. It has a transforming effect upon those who are exposed to its influence. The apostles of Christ were men of extraordinary vision. Jesus' declaration of intent lived in their minds and hearts:

I will build my church. . . (Mt 16:18).

They saw Christianity not as a mere offshoot of Judaism with its headquarters in Jerusalem, but as something with a unique identity of its own which would grow until it filled the whole earth. But each had their perspective on how it would come about and knew the part they were to play. Between them they exercised a diversity of ministries which reflected their personal visions.

Peter, breaking with tradition, shared the gospel with some non-Jews and thereby set a precedent for future action (Acts 11:1–21). Paul assembled a small team of helpers and set off on a series of missionary journeys which led to the founding of a whole string of churches, strategically placed to extend their influence.

These men had to define the nature of their vision, for their own sakes as much as anyone else's, and from time to time they also had to defend it (Acts 15:1–21).

Since then there have been many others, men and women, visionary leaders who have inspired others to follow them and achieve great things for the cause of Christ. The Wesley brothers, John and Charles, established Methodism. William Booth founded the Salvation Army. The diminutive Gladys Aylward promoted a great Christian work in China. George Müller built and ran a group of homes for orphaned children.

True leaders have this visionary outlook as part of their disposition. Check yourself against this requirement by completing the following questionnaire, circling the number in the column that best describes you.

VISION TEST

	Always	Often	Seldom	Never
You consider new angles and ideas until your vision becomes clear.	4	3	2	1
You translate the vision into a simple form that others can readily grasp.	4	3	2	1
You inspire others to embrace the vision.	4	3	2	1
You make contact at all levels within your organisation.	4	3	2	1
You are warm and supportive.	4	3	2	1
Your vision is an all-important cause for you and you instil this belief in others.	4	3	2	1
You concentrate on the major strengths of your people and of the organisation.	4	3	2	1
You measure the ongoing success of your vision.	4	3	2	1

A score of 24 or less shows the need for some improvement.

The leader must do two things in relation to his or her vision.

1. Vision must be *shaped*. It may begin as the glimmer of an idea, but it has to be fleshed out until it has substance and meaning and can be talked about, planned for and worked towards.
2. Vision must be *shared*. It has to be communicated in a convincing way so that others affected by it will 'own' it and work enthusiastically to see it fulfilled. More will be said about this in the next chapter.

Shaping the vision

Shaping a vision requires first that you *define* it. As a leader you have to determine what your vision is. There are almost as many different kinds of vision as there are leaders. This should come as no surprise, but whatever its form there are three things about the leader's vision which are important:

- It should be *clear*, that is, capable of being understood and communicated.
- It should be *specific*, that is, capable of being targeted and achieved.
- Above all, it should be *correct*.

There are times when well-intentioned leaders, perhaps from the best of motives, decide to pursue the wrong things. As a result, people are led in the wrong direction. Time, effort and resources are expended needlessly, often with regrettable consequences:

If a blind man leads a blind man, both will fall into a pit (Mt 15:14).

How does the leader get his or her vision? Suppose you've just been given the job of Sunday school superintendent at your local church, or you've been appointed to head up a team of outreach workers in your area, and you realise the unique opportunity this presents to shape your part of the organisation. You want to present a compelling vision. So, what do you do? Go to the mountain top? Solicit 'vision input' from your team?

Moses' revelation in the desert set in motion events leading to the famous freedom trek out of Egypt and saw him emerge as a political and spiritual leader, achieving lofty aims against incredible odds, changing the course of history and putting his stamp on an entire civilisation.

The vision Moses had concerning the future of the people he was to lead began with God:

The Lord said, 'I have indeed seen the misery of my people in Egypt. I have heard them crying out because of their

slave drivers, and I am concerned about their suffering. So I have come down to rescue them from the hand of the Egyptians and to bring them up out of that land into a good and spacious land, a land flowing with milk and honey. . . So now, go. I am sending you to Pharaoh to bring my people the Israelites out of Egypt' (Exod 3:7–10).

Moses listened as God spoke, and the vision which was to change the rest of his life and the lives of those who followed him was born. This vision clarified over a period of time, taking shape as he pondered its implications and as more details were added. But essentially, it began with an idea which God put in his mind.

This is an important starting point for all Christian leaders. The words of the Apostle Paul, applicable to the entire population of Christians, are of particular relevance to leaders:

'No eye has seen, no ear has heard, no mind has conceived what God has prepared for those who love him'—but God has revealed it to us by his Spirit (1 Cor 2:9–10a).

Here are some additional things you can do which will help you to determine your vision.

Pay attention to your past experiences. You've been part of the organisation, or some organisation, for years. What have you learned? Ask yourself, 'If I could rewrite the history of my own achievements or of the church or organisation, what would I change?' What has been memorable? What has worked? What hasn't worked?

Allow your ideas to clarify over a period of time. Make notes; write ideas down, loosely or precisely. Think about one component at a time over a period of days or even weeks. You might consider your people—the capabilities and skills they represent, the relationships they sustain. Or, your potential as an organisation—where could you be in five, ten or twenty years' time? What are other, similar organisations or churches doing? Are there trends that are changing the way things work? Do they represent opportunities or threats?

Talk to others. Curiously enough, visions are seldom original. Two modern management writers observe:

> The leader may have been the one who chose the image from those available at the moment, articulated it, gave it form and legitimacy and focused attention on it but the leader was rarely the one who conceived of it in the first place (*Leaders*, Bennis and Nanus).

So listen, ask, swap stories, chat about your ideas. Pay attention, especially to those who are advocating new or different things.

A second step towards shaping the vision is to *develop* it from the idea stage to the point where it can be made to reflect the goals and strategies needed to fulfil it. Leaders need time to think and meditate, mulling over ideas and concepts, letting them take shape and grow. Through this process the leader sees goals emerge. He or she also begins to sense the kind of strategies needed to implement the changes envisaged.

This development stage is sometimes called 'scenario-building'. Try it. It is perfectly possible to construct several different scenarios—outlines which depict ways in which your vision might work out. You can play these onto the screen of your mind and observe the outcomes. If you find you think in 'boxes', use a flip chart or dry-wipe board to assist the thinking process.

It's possible that the Apostle Paul engaged in scenario-building soon after his remarkable conversion to Christ on the road to Damascus. Referring to the time spent in the deserts of Arabia he recalls:

> **When God, who set me apart from birth and called me by his grace, was pleased to reveal his Son in me so that I might preach him among the Gentiles, I did not consult any man, nor did I go up to Jerusalem to see those who were apostles before I was, but I went immediately into Arabia and later returned to Damascus (Gal 1:15–17).**

There, in the solitary wilderness, he had time to think. His ideas had time to grow. But, more significantly, there is a strong inference that during this time he, like Moses, was hearing from God, and as he contemplated the way ahead his vision of God's purpose surely began to crystallise.

As a Christian leader you will find it helpful to engage in the process of scenario-building as you try to develop your vision. Here are some guidelines:

Provide yourself with a simple yet thorough description of your vision, including its spiritual dimension, strategic direction and core values. This is sometimes called a vision or mission statement. It is good to try and state this using no more than about twenty-five words.

A well-written statement will provide direction and guidance for you and the team you are leading. It will clarify your purpose and meaning. By referring to it and by internalising its meaning you are more likely to choose behaviours that serve your values and reject those that oppose them. When writing your vision or mission statement, remember that it is as much a process of discovery as it is of creation. Don't rush the process or set rigid timetables for yourself. Rather, go slowly and ask yourself the right questions and think deeply about your values and aspirations.

Next, make a thorough evaluation of the factors involved in implementing your vision and put special emphasis on those which can determine success or failure. This kind of evaluation is sometimes known as a SWOT analysis. SWOT stands for Strengths, Weaknesses, Opportunities and Threats.

A *strength* is something that is going well or something you and your team are good at.

A *weakness* is something that's going badly or something that you and your team aren't good at.

An *opportunity* is something that may benefit you if you act.

A *threat* is something that may harm you if you don't act.

In carrying out a SWOT analysis of your leadership situation you should (a) list all the strengths, weaknesses, opportunities and threats that you can think of, and (b) review the lists and decide on the kind of actions you will take to:

- Exploit strengths by building them up; applying them to other areas; publicising them.
- Combat weaknesses by correcting them; reducing reliance on them.
- Exploit opportunities by acting so that they're more likely to happen; maximise the benefits if they do happen.
- Combat threats by acting so that they're less likely to occur; acting so as to minimise the damage if they do occur.

Rank your proposed actions into high, medium or low priority.

Finally, identify the milestones or major events which should occur as you implement your vision. Sequence these in logical progression.

No precise path to finding a vision can be described and the subject is too important to be trivialised by books and articles explaining 'how to get vision' in ten easy steps. The process of finding an appropriate vision for your organisation is highly personal, but there are some pointers to be gained from others' experience. The following may prove helpful:

- Maintain the right attitude: focus on God.
- Fill the mind with proper thoughts and concepts.
- Face the future and forget the past. 'Life can only be understood backwards but it has to be lived forwards' (Søren Kierkegaard).
- Fail constructively. Be prepared to learn from mistakes and not to be discouraged by them.

Finally, here are some important checks against which to test the effectiveness of your vision.

Vision must:

- Be different. It should challenge people. Edwin H. Land, founder of Polaroid, said: 'The first thing you do is teach the person to feel that the undertaking is manifestly important and nearly impossible. That draws out the drives that make people strong.'

- Make sense. It should be clear and understandable and be recognised as consistent with the realities of the current situation.
- Be well articulated. It has to be expressed in convincing ways.
- Be lived by the leader. He must show he believes in it passionately.
- Be the work of others. They must 'own' it and promote it.

KEY POINTS SUMMARY

The significance of vision emphasised as the essential starting point for leadership.

Steps to defining and subsequently developing vision outlined.

Scenario-building as a means of developing vision.

Checks to make on the effectiveness of vision.

GUIDES FOR ACTION

Produce a vision or mission statement for your part of the organisation of twenty-five words or less. Carry out a SWOT analysis—looking at strengths, weaknesses, opportunities and threats which feature in your present leadership situation.

Chapter Eight

IMPLEMENTING THE VISION

The only way to lead people is to show them a future: a leader is a dealer in hope.

Napoleon Bonaparte

Follow me. . . and I will make you fishers of men (Mt 4:19).

Write down the [vision] and make it plain. . . so that a herald may run with it (Hab 2:2).

Leadership is shaping and sharing a vision which gives point to the work of others.

Charles B. Handy

New words do not always signify new ideas. Sometimes they are just a cover for the old, making it look and sound different. Even so, this is not simply a chapter about the principles of good communication. Its key purpose is to highlight the need to communicate the leadership vision or manifesto effectively.

There is more to communicating than getting others to the point where they say, 'I know what you mean.' Effective communication moves people to the place where they say, 'I'll do something about it.' Leaders have to share their vision in ways that will get others to 'own' it and commit themselves to working for its fulfilment.

Suppose you are the leader of a small Christian group and you have a vision that will affect their future. The dimensions of it are clear to you; now you have to share it with them in a way that will gain their enthusiasm and support. You need to:

- Generate an understanding of it.
- Gain acceptance for it.
- Get your people to 'own' it and commit themselves to it.

How are you to do this?

Research shows that a disproportionately large volume of the communications which occur among people takes place by non-verbal means. The following diagram illustrates how understanding occurs:

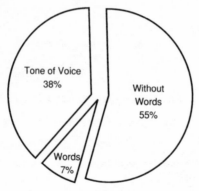

Experience bears it out also: people communicate by what they say but more significantly by what they do and by what they are:

You. . . are our letter. . . known and read by everybody (2 Cor 3:2).

It has to be added that people read the words and actions of their leaders with particular closeness.

There are two fundamental ways of sharing a vision with others. The first is to *live* it—passionately and consistently. The second is to *articulate* it—clearly and at every opportunity, explaining it and exhorting others to act upon it. The leader has to do both.

Living the vision: You have to do this day in and day out. Your thoughts must be trained upon it, your words should draw attention to it, your actions should be geared onto it. Your vision will reflect the values you hold and the desires you have, so the example you set should be the kind which projects these clearly and consistently. More will be said about 'living the vision' in a later chapter.

Articulating the vision: This means you have to talk about it frequently. Take every opportunity that comes your way to explain it and exhort others in relation to it. Use these opportunities wisely; don't be a bore. Winston Churchill once defined a fanatic as 'someone who can't change his mind and won't change the subject'!

The visionary leader is constantly 'campaigning', in this total sense, for the wholehearted support and energy of others.

The process of communicating a vision has three notable phases. The diagram below illustrates these and uses a scale which runs from -10 to -1 in order to track the followers' responses.

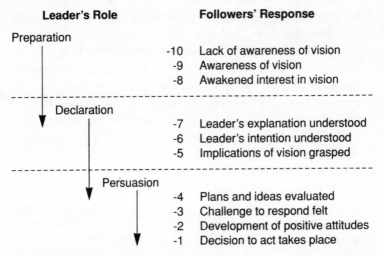

Leader's Role		Followers' Response
Preparation		
	-10	Lack of awareness of vision
	-9	Awareness of vision
	-8	Awakened interest in vision
Declaration		
	-7	Leader's explanation understood
	-6	Leader's intention understood
	-5	Implications of vision grasped
Persuasion		
	-4	Plans and ideas evaluated
	-3	Challenge to respond felt
	-2	Development of positive attitudes
	-1	Decision to act takes place

This approach can serve as a model for building up a comprehensive strategy simply and quickly in order to communicate understanding of, and gain support for, the vision or manifesto. It includes coping with the negative emotions of others; incorporating consideration for viewpoints of others; overcoming resistance when presenting new concepts or proposing changes in direction or culture; giving others help in making decisions about what is being put to them.

Phase one: preparation

This is very much the time for proving your ideas and for gaining feedback about them. There is a certain amount of 'testing the temperature' that can go on. You can talk informally about ideas. Information can be gathered which will help you to mould your approach. This phase is characterised by action and experimentation rather than analysis and planning. Its purpose is to give the vision a certain 'presence' by creating an awareness of it and by awakening interest in it.

Nehemiah made this his first priority:

I went to Jerusalem, and after staying there three days I set out during the night with a few men. I had not told anyone what my God had put in my heart to do for Jerusalem. . . By night I went out through the Valley Gate towards the Jackal Well and the Dung Gate, examining the walls of Jerusalem, which had been broken down, and its gates, which had been destroyed by fire. Then I moved on towards the Fountain Gate and the King's Pool, but there was not enough room for my mount to get through; so I went up the valley by night, examining the wall. Finally, I turned back and re-entered through the Valley Gate. The officials did not know where I had gone or what I was doing, because as yet I had said nothing to the Jews or the priests or nobles or officials or any others who would be doing the work (Neh 2:11–16).

People are seldom ready for new ideas, especially those which lead to change. They need time to absorb them. New concepts have to be sown and nurtured carefully.

'Live it' first, then 'preach it' afterwards. These are the keys. Begin with a formal declaration and you are doomed! For one thing, you may not have sufficient understanding of what you are trying to do in the early stages and you're likely to be trapped by a thousand small inconsistencies as you wobble towards clarity.

Concentrate on getting the concept into the bloodstream of your organisation. Do this before calling any church meetings or posting any slogans or circulating any notes. These can come later. It's better to wallow in ideas first, then as things become clear, begin to live them out. This gets the process started. When the time for explaining and planning and implementing programmes of action arrives, things will already be moving in the right direction.

Phase two: declaration

Then I said to them, 'You see the trouble we are in: Jerusalem lies in ruins, and its gates have been burned with fire. Come, let us rebuild the wall of Jerusalem, and we will no longer be in disgrace' (Neh 2:17).

This is the disclosure phase, where intentions are declared and proposals for action are made known. It is also when the nature of the vision and plans for fulfilling it start to be articulated in formal and extremely focused ways. The chief purpose is to get people to appreciate the issues at stake and to grasp the implications for themselves.

There are a few key things you should keep in mind as you prepare to share details of your vision and the plan for achieving it with others. The letters of the word 'POEM' will help to remind you of what they are—Purpose, Others, Effect and Method.

Purpose: Be clear about the precise purpose of each message you communicate. Ask yourself, 'What do I want to say?' Try and sum it up in twenty-five words or less.

Others: Think about the people you'll be communicating with. How much do they know already? What kind of language are they likely to understand and appreciate? Are they simple, sophisticated, intellectually strong? Have they any prejudices? How are they likely to react?

Here are six important points to consider in relation to the people you're dealing with:

- The people you meet feel they are important and want to be respected. They may be thinking about other things as you approach and may feel emotional about them or about being disturbed.
- The people you meet will always look at your ideas from their viewpoint.
- People will only be interested in your idea if they first see how they will benefit from it.
- People want facts about your idea. They are seldom influenced by arguments or bragging.
- Others have a right to their opinions, be they right or wrong, and these must be respected.
- People sometimes need help in making a decision about your idea.

These points are developed further at the end of this section in a way that will assist you to plan your own strategy for communicating with your people.

Effect: What do you want people to do after you have communicated with them? How do you want them to respond?

There are four important aspects of a message which are always communicated, and it's worth keeping them in mind as you plan the effect you want your communication to have:

1. Sense—factual meaning. For example, 'The church is going to be rehoused in a new building'; 'The prayer group is going to meet twice each week for the next three months'; 'The bookshop is going to open another branch.'
2. Feelings—what the communicator actually feels about the facts of the message. For example, enthusiasm for the concept; concern about a failure to act; caution over how something is to be implemented.
3. Tone—indicating the relationship between the communicator and the recipients of the information. For example, 'I am the

leader and you must do what I'm saying'; 'I'm seeking your
views as those who have experience in doing this kind of work.'
4. Personality—self-image. For example, overbearing; reasonable; sincere; selfish.

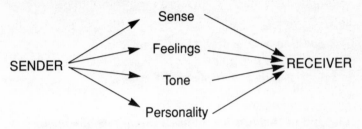

It's easy to see how misunderstandings occur! The chief problem
lies in being able to communicate sensibly without, at the same
time, sending any contradictory signals. Often the best of efforts
are frustrated because the receiver's perceptions don't match the
sender's intentions.

The converse is also true. Communication is more effective
where the emotional, tonal and personal components are seen to
be complementing the coherent, well-structured presentation of
facts.

Barriers to Communication

This diagram illustrates some of the obstacles that are nearly
always present in any communication scenario:

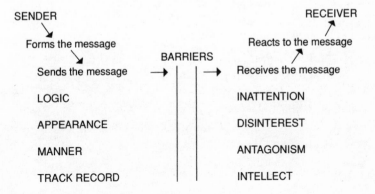

Some barriers are created by the senders themselves, starting with an inability to form the message correctly and continuing with a failure to communicate it effectively for one or a combination of several reasons. Likewise, the recipients may not comprehend the message as it was intended that they should, either because they cannot or will not. Beyond this lies the further question of how they will respond to it.

Christian leaders should remember that all of the foregoing is overlaid by a spiritual dimension. There is a negative aspect to this:

The god of this age has blinded the minds of unbelievers, so that they cannot see the light of the gospel of the glory of Christ (2 Cor 4:4).

There are spiritual forces at work whose aim is to wreck the communication process by causing confusion, dissuasion, intellectual blindness and so on. This can affect both sender and receiver. There is also a strongly positive aspect, epitomised by the words of the Apostle Paul:

My message and my preaching were not with wise and persuasive words, but with a demonstration of the Spirit's power (1 Cor 2:4).

The Christian leader, aware of the communication barriers that exist, and the need to make a conscious effort to overcome them, should also bear in mind the positive and negative aspects of the spiritual dimension which is always present when he or she is trying to communicate.

Method: Which method will you adopt in order to get your message across? Should you write or speak? Is there an order in which you should communicate with others? Are there established channels you need to use? Whatever you decide, here is a plan that will help you to create a climate of understanding and acceptance of your vision among those with whom you are sharing the details.

A six-point plan for improving communications effectiveness

1. Remember: The people you meet feel they are important and want to be respected. They may be thinking about other things as you approach and may feel emotional about them or about being disturbed.

You can counter the negative feelings you may cause as you interrupt their train of thought or you can calm any other negative feelings they may have, now or at any later time, by using these 'emotion movers':

Mood and manner	Your mood and manner will depend on lots of things, eg, frame of mind, appearance, facial expression, tone of voice, actions and reactions, the use you make of your surroundings.
Friendly questions	If you are to use these effectively you have to know enough about your hearers so as to put questions naturally and sincerely.
Good turn	You can find ways of doing good turns for people if you know their objectives and needs and if you study your contacts with them.
Contacts	Contacts can be established with people through experiences, associations or interests and mutual friends.
Assurance	You can give people assurance through honest affirmation or encouragement.
Personal prestige	You can use personal prestige by mentioning modestly any past experience which indicates to others that they can rely on you.

2. Remember: The people you meet will always look at your ideas from their viewpoint.

Their viewpoint will depend largely on what they want from their life and from the work they are engaged in.

You will be able to appreciate how people will look at your ideas if you study their actions and learn their objectives.

Their goals, ambitions and desires are their objectives. If you know their objectives you can organise your thinking so that you can explain how your idea will help them achieve their aims.

3. Remember: People will only be interested in your idea if they first see how they will benefit from it.

Most folk will respond positively to what you want them to do if they see how they will benefit.

Sometimes people are unaware of the conditions they face which, together with the way they act, are causing them, or could cause them, to lose out. At other times they are aware of these conditions, but think they can do nothing about them and so become complacent.

You can lead people to appreciate how these losses are hindering them from realising their goals. By asking 'condition' questions, you can start them thinking and talking about the conditions they face. By asking 'loss' questions, you can get them to admit losses and establish in their minds the need for benefits.

4. Remember: People want facts about your idea. They are seldom influenced by arguments or bragging.

If people want to see an improvement in their situation they will be willing to listen to reason.

You can appeal to people's reason by using these 'reason movers':

Benefit	The desirable results people will get from your idea.
Good quality	The features of your idea, or how it works.
Poor quality	An idea or approach that is inferior to yours in that it is less effective in solving the problem, changing the situation or

	achieving the goal.
Loss	The undesirable results people would get by using or sticking with the poor quality approach.
Prestige	Statements that show other people's approval of your idea.
Story	Quoting what others who have benefited from your idea or suffered losses from some other idea, have said.

You can appeal to reason by combining these 'reason movers' in four types of statement:

Reason why	Benefit/Good quality
Comparison	Benefit/Good quality/Poor quality/Loss
Conclusion	Benefit/Good quality/Poor quality/Loss
Evidence	Benefit/Good quality/Prestige/Story

5. Remember: Others have a right to their opinions, be they right or wrong, and these must be respected.

The opinions of your hearers will often differ from your own. Often they will object to your idea or certain things about it.

Never assume that an idea is being accepted simply because an objection is not automatically voiced. If people fail to indicate a reaction you should test for it.

When people object to your idea, remember they will probably defend their objection emotionally. So, before you attempt to overcome their objection you should quieten their emotions. There are three ways to do this:

- Show by your mood and manner that you consider the other person(s) important and that you respect them.
- Show that you understand their viewpoint and that you intend to be reasonable in discussing it, by repeating a key thought or giving assurance.
- If necessary, further assure your listener(s) by showing why and how you understand their viewpoint.

The resistance you encounter can generally be classed as one or a combination of the following obstacles:

Obstacle	Key 'mover' to use
Habit	Benefit
Fear	Good quality
Cost	Benefit
Complaint	Good quality action, benefit, explanation—demonstration
Competition	Questions and comparison statements
	Conditions, loss, benefit
Lack of information	Strong emotion movers
Difficult personality	Good quality actions
Time	Strong emotion movers

6. Remember: People sometimes need help in making a decision about your idea.

There are several ways of helping people to reach a decision. Use a question to see if they want the benefits you have mentioned.

Use a command as a direct, courteous request suggesting that they accept. Reassure them of the benefits. Give them the opportunity to make a split decision, ie, where it is possible offer them two choices, either of which constitutes acceptance. Summarise the benefits.

There are no gimmicky solutions to human relations and communications situations. You must investigate and analyse the conditions which you and your team face before you speak or act. Plan your communications wisely and use good judgement.

Phase three: persuasion

Another important aspect of communicating a vision is to do it in ways that will get others to 'own' it and commit themselves to its

fulfilment. This phase is characterised by discussion, the evaluation of plans and ideas, the development of positive attitudes and
the decision to act.

Following his declaration of intent Nehemiah sought the
support of others so that his vision might become a reality:

**I also told them about the gracious hand of my God upon
me and what the king had said to me. They replied, 'Let us
start rebuilding.' So they began this good work (Neh 2:18).**

How does the leader get others to 'pick up the ball and run with
it'? The process of gaining 'ownership' and commitment is one
that can be managed.

How to manage commitment

There are three basic steps you can and should take as a leader in
order to gain the active support and involvement of your people.

First, *promote a sense of belonging to your church or
organisation*. This is crucial. If people feel that they don't belong
they will never become committed. John Biffen, the highly
respected and articulate leader of the House of Commons, was a
member of Mrs Thatcher's Cabinet during the 1980s. However,
he was described by Bernard Ingham, the Prime Minister's Press
Secretary, as 'semi-detached' from the government. He never
really belonged and was sacked in 1987.

Similarly, there are people of whom it may justly be said that
they are 'in the church but not of it'! Whether this is the result of
some deliberate act on their part or is simply a matter of default
is not important. The fact remains that such folk are never
committed. But as a leader you can take steps to foster this all-
important sense of belonging if you:

Keep people informed by	thorough regular briefings;
	practising a policy of open dis-closure;
	presenting information in ways that can be readily understood.

| Keep people involved by | playing down the idea of status and the use of status symbols; taking their feelings and views into account. |
| Share success with them by | learning to celebrate good results; letting them share the benefits. |

Next, *promote a sense of excitement about the task in hand.* The Old Testament leader Nehemiah wrote these words in his diary:

We rebuilt the wall till all of it reached half its height, for the people worked with all their heart (Neh 4:6).

Three things will help to produce this sense of excitement about the job:

Create pride by	giving responsibility for quality; identifying people with the outcomes of their work.
Create trust by	giving decision making responsibility to those doing the work.
Create accountability by	setting challenging targets and letting people feel responsible for getting results.

Third, *promote confidence in your leadership.* The plaintive words of Jesus, spoken to the Twelve at a time when many were deciding not to follow him any longer, hint at a crisis of leadership which was taking place just then:

'You do not want to leave too, do you?' Jesus asked the Twelve (Jn 6:67).

The reply shows that confidence in the leader produces commitment:

Simon Peter answered him, 'Lord, to whom shall we go? You have the words of eternal life. We believe and know that you are the Holy One of God' (Jn 6: 68–69).

You can promote confidence in your leadership by:

- Exercising authority in appropriate ways.
- Showing dedication.
- Displaying your competence as a leader.

The virtuous circle

Giving members of your team a sense of belonging is an essential ingredient in gaining their commitment. But this in itself may not always be enough to guarantee their full support. People also need to feel a sense of excitement about what they are doing. This second pillar of commitment can be established by an appeal to three higher level needs: pride—that is, in the work because it is seen and felt to be worthwhile—trust and accountability for results.

Someone who is trusted and has pride in the work they are doing—'a job that's worth doing is worth doing well'—will increasingly want to accept responsibility.

All of the foregoing, when allied with confidence in the leadership, becomes a 'virtuous circle' which strengthens personal motivation and leads to greater commitment. Leaders who can bring this about may justly claim to have communicated their vision effectively.

KEY POINTS SUMMARY

Leaders need to share their vision in ways that will get others to 'own' it and become committed to supporting the fulfilment of it.

The process of communicating a vision to others has three notable phases: preparation, declaration and persuasion.

Most communication occurs by non-verbal means.

There are numerous barriers to effective communication which are set up by the 'sender' as well as by the 'receiver' of information. These have to be noted and overcome.

Study your communications closely. The six-point plan for

improving communications effectiveness will help you to develop the right kind of strategy for getting others to understand and accept your vision.

Get others to 'own' the vision by managing the commitment process carefully:

- Create a sense of belonging.
- Create a sense of excitement.
- Create a sense of confidence.

GUIDE FOR ACTION

Select an issue or topic which is key to your leadership vision. Use the six-point plan to develop an effective communication strategy for getting it understood and accepted by your group.

Use the three-phase concept of *preparation*, *declaration* and *persuasion* to gauge the current status of your implementation programme.

Chapter Nine

FUNCTIONING AS A ROLE MODEL

The way to gain a good reputation is to endeavour to be what you desire to appear.

Socrates

Be their ideal; let them follow the way you teach and live; be a pattern for them in your love, your faith and your clean thoughts (1 Tim 4:12, TLB).

Behavioural scientists tell us with rare accord that 'modelling' is one of the primary ways in which people learn. This may explain why, amid the confusion and uncertainty of the present day when the need to pursue the right agenda is all important, so many people look instinctively for role models to guide them.

In his classic *Study of History*, Arnold Toynbee speaks of 'mimesis', the process by which people mimic their leaders. Inevitably, people in your group, church or Christian organisation will watch you, the leader. Like it or not, what you do and how you do it—not what you 'sermonise' about—will become their preoccupation. Yours is the pattern they will adopt. By direct and indirect means their agenda will come to mirror your own. The clearer the signal you send, the greater will be your effectiveness as a role model.

Perhaps now more than ever, leaders have to lead by personal example. Ultimately it is the actions of the leader which provide a living model of his or her strategic vision.

Leading is a symbolic activity. It involves energising people to do new things—things which they may previously have thought to be unimportant. Your personal energy and intensity, or lack of it, will send a signal to others about the extent to which you are in earnest about these same issues.

The value of values

Have you ever gone into a restaurant, taken a look at the surroundings, then quickly left, thinking, 'I'm not eating in here!'? Perhaps you were put off by the lack of cleanliness or the demeanour of the staff. Compare this to entering a really high-class establishment which boasts gourmet food, a spotless appearance and an international chef, and finding that they won't let you in because you're not wearing a suit and tie! The issue in both cases is the same: values.

Values are a means by which people in organisations communicate to outsiders and each other key messages about themselves. Values may be personal to an individual or shared by the group. Either way they provide a measure of the worth given to things and they help to sift the important from the unimportant in individual or corporate life.

Everyone has values of some sort. These derive mainly from three sources:

Moral and spiritual, relating to a sense of right and wrong and to deeply-held beliefs and convictions.

Rational and intellectual, relating to reason, logic and common sense.

Experience of life: largely pragmatic and based on an understanding of the way things are likely to work out in practice, regardless of other considerations.

Most people's values are drawn from one or a combination of all three sources. A conflict of values can occur within an individual and often this cannot be sustained for long. The Apostle Paul records:

Demas, because he loved this world, has deserted me (2 Tim 4:10).

Sadly, there are many who profess one set of values but live by another. The scathing remarks which Jesus directed at some of the religious leaders of his day are a testimony to this:

Woe to you Pharisees, because you give God a tenth of your mint, rue and all other kinds of garden herbs, but you neglect justice and the love of God. You should have practised the latter without leaving the former undone (Lk 11:42).

Whether consistent or inconsistent, conscious or unconscious, real or professed, our values are strong determinants of our behaviour. They determine what we regard as worthwhile and right. They form the standards by which we judge ourselves and others, including our feelings and attitudes towards our fellows, our purposes in life, the systems we value, the ideas and principles we can accept.

There is a serious question which every leader should ask of himself, namely: What are the values that guide my life and by which I lead my team?

The Bible is teeming with value statements that are deeply suggestive:

You shall have no other gods before me.
You shall not make for yourself an idol in the form of anything in heaven above or on the earth beneath...
You shall not misuse the name of the Lord your God...
Remember the Sabbath day by keeping it holy...
Honour your father and your mother...
You shall not murder.
You shall not commit adultery.
You shall not steal.
You shall not give false testimony against your neighbour.
You shall not covet... (Exod 20:3–17).

Do not store up for yourselves treasures on earth, where moth and rust destroy, and where thieves break in and steal. But store up for yourselves treasures in heaven, where moth and rust do not destroy, and where thieves do not break in and steal. For where your treasure is, there your heart will be also (Mt 6:19–21).

Now the overseer must be above reproach, the husband of but one wife, temperate, self-controlled, respectable, hospitable, able to teach, not given to drunkenness, not violent but gentle, not quarrelsome, not a lover of money. He must manage his own family well and see that his children obey him with proper respect. (If anyone does not know how to manage his own family, how can he take care of God's church?) He must not be a recent convert, or he may become conceited and fall under the same judgment as the devil. He must also have a good reputation with outsiders, so that he will not fall into disgrace and into the devil's trap (1 Tim 3:2–7).

Thus values provide the boundaries: within an organisation they determine what is prized, what is to be pursued and what will be punished or rewarded. Above all, an organisation's values define what its highest priorities really are.

Leaders need to be clear about their own personal values and about those of the organisation, church or group within which they serve. It is useful to bear in mind that people generally only practise what they believe. They may state their beliefs loudly, often and with considerable eloquence, but if, in the final analysis, they don't ever do what they say, then this usually means that they don't really believe it. This point is of particular importance for leaders because values determine not only actions but vision. A leader's stated vision should reflect his or her values because it is the things they deeply and truly care about, the vital concerns, that will eventually surface.

For example, there is little point in setting out to enhance the quality and profile of prayer within your church if you personally don't have prayer as a high priority on your agenda.

Some churches and organisations have written constitutions which reflect the values they respect and have chosen to abide by. These are its declared or intended values. 'Articles of Faith' and 'Mission Statements' are further examples of the same thing. But within most groups there is also an unwritten, informal set of values at work. These reveal themselves by the way in which things tend to work out in practice.

Here are some of the ways in which you can find out what your organisation's values are:

1. Ask: 'On what grounds might a person be removed from the job they are doing within your team or church?'
2. Look for things that make people mad then ask them why they got that way!
3. Look carefully at what distinguishes you from other churches or from other similar Christian organisations.
4. Ask someone who is new to your team or organisation for their views on the above issues.
5. Go back to your roots. Look at those who founded the organisation and try to identify their values.
6. Bring a group of leaders who operate at one level in, say, your church, together in a working environment with leaders from other levels and see what happens!
7. Imagine yourself ten years from now. What would you look back on with the greatest satisfaction?
8. Values often become clear when the issue is presented in a yes/no way:

   'Is the customer always right?'
   'Will we go to any lengths to raise money for our new church building?'
   'Are we to treat the customer with a small account just as we treat those with large accounts?'

This kind of simplified exercise shows how values evolve, take shape and ultimately breathe life into the organisation's vision. Values direct the daily life and actions of its members and bring these into line with its chosen goals.

Perhaps the importance of values to an organisation can best be understood by observing what happens when they don't exist. No values usually means no vision—no common bond, no shared intent, no understood goal. This is a recipe for chaos and confusion and the eventual slump into oblivion. Values are like lights in a dark room. Without them you're likely to spend a lot of time bumping into walls.

Vision and values are interrelated. Vision is shaped by values, and values come alive through vision. When people start to pursue a vision they find themselves living out the things they truly believe in.

The power of shared values

Edmund Burke, elder statesman and political writer, observed:

> Men cannot act with effect unless they act in concert; men cannot act in concert who do not act with confidence; men cannot act with confidence who are not bound together with common opinions, common affections and common interests.

If people are to work together effectively they must have a set of shared beliefs. These beliefs, sometimes called 'core' values, are the things upon which all are agreed. They are 'bottom line' issues which lie right at the heart of effective performance.

General de Gaulle said of his wartime ally Sir Winston Churchill: 'We both navigated by the same stars.'

When properly selected, values can do the following things:

- Create an atmosphere of common purpose and trust.
- Provide clear focus for giving and receiving feedback and for reviewing performance.
- Help everyone to know or set priorities.
- Simplify rules and policies.
- Help everyone to understand what is expected of them.
- Provide guidelines for selecting and training new people.

- Help to avoid 'flavour of the month' activities and the resulting waste of energies and shift of priorities.

These values need to be supported by people who have the skills to make them work. As a rule, leaders don't create core values. They discover active or dormant beliefs that they and a critical mass of potential followers care about. Then they shape these into a focus for energy. They do this by becoming role models: this releases the power of example. The most effective role model for expressing values is contained in just six words: '*Do anything you see me doing.*'

There are three powerful ways in which you send signals to others about yourself, your values and your leadership vision. These ways are as practical as they are powerful.

Let everyone see where your priorities lie

A sure means of doing this is to let it show in the way you spend your time. Look at your diary and examine your commitments carefully. Are you spending the right amount of time on the right things? How much time are you spending on the issues that you claim are important?

Priorities—everyone has them. As a rule, the amount of time and effort you spend on something reflects the degree of importance you have assigned to it. You can decide the kind of message you want your diary of commitments to send. Nehemiah sent a clear message to all and sundry during a key stage of the building project he was involved in:

Sanballat and Geshem sent me this message: 'Come, let us meet together in one of the villages on the plain of Ono.' But they were scheming to harm me; so I sent messengers to them with this reply: 'I am carrying on a great project and cannot go down. Why should the work stop while I leave it and go down to you?' Four times they sent me the same message, and each time I gave them the same answer (Neh 6:2–4).

What matters is that everyone who works for you and with you sees you embracing the topic with both arms and with your diary! The real message to others is contained in the amount of time you are seen to be spending on the issue.

Exploit the power of your actions

'Actions speak louder than words' is a truism which has universal application. With leaders this is especially so and you should never underestimate the power of even your smallest action. Each day is marked by hundreds of symbolic acts on your part. Whether you are conscious of these is another matter. The fact is they combine to give members of your team a clear picture of your true concerns.

Get into the habit of considering the symbolic significance of your actions—people close to you are thirsty for clues about your priorities! Here are some questions you could ask yourself:

1. 'Can I point to one symbolic activity each day, which shows that I am solidly in support of my top priority?' Remember this: trust and credibility develop as others note your 'symbolic' integrity, not your 'policy' statements.
2. 'What kind of questions do I ask first?' You talk about the need to recognise the importance of every individual and to help them fulfil their role, but the first questions you ask are always about things, new equipment, funds or, projects. Your priorities are clear to everyone.
3. 'What contacts do I make? Who do I visit?' For example, you say that developing strong links with other churches in your area is the key to a successful partnership in spreading the gospel. But your diary shows that you've had little contact with other ministers and there are few signs that you've made any attempt to become involved in the occasional get-together.

Whether you tackle this inevitable set of signals opportunistically is up to you, but be assured of this: you will send them, and others will make a pattern from them. Lay hold of these opportunities; exploit the power of even your smallest actions. You are a rich, daily pattern to others and you can manage it to positive good effect.

A third way to project yourself as a role model is to:

Let the choices you make about people reflect your priorities

When there is a job of work to be done who do you pick to do it? That choice will say a lot about you and your forward plan. Are you 'playing it safe', maintaining the status quo, or are you being adventurous, even to the point of taking risks with the appointment of some people?

The twelve apostles were not selected carelessly or at random. But neither were they the obvious, safe choices considering what Christ had in mind. The men he surrounded himself with, in whom he chose to invest himself and to whom he eventually entrusted his work, had few credentials. In many ways they represented a radical (some might even have said risky) choice. They also represented, as events later showed, the correct choice—even the selection of Judas Iscariot was not a mistake (Jn 17:12). However, the making of such choices required not only discernment but a certain amount of boldness and faith in people.

In making choices about people the Christian leader has first to try and discern God's choice and then ensure that this is reflected in what he or she does:

One of those days Jesus went out to a mountainside to pray, and spent the night praying to God. When morning came, he called his disciples to him and chose twelve of them, whom he also designated apostles (Lk 6:12–13).

Additionally, leaders have to remember that God's choice does not always follow conventional wisdom:

When they arrived Samuel saw Eliab and thought, 'Surely the Lord's anointed stands here before the Lord.'

But the Lord said to Samuel, 'Do not consider his appearance or his height, for I have rejected him. The

Lord does not look at the things man looks at. Man looks at the outward appearance, but the Lord looks at the heart' (1 Sam 16:6–7).

The kind of choices you make about people, whether selecting them for certain jobs, giving them more or different responsibilities, moving them sidewards or getting rid of them altogether, will draw attention to several things—about you. For one thing, it will highlight the seriousness of your intentions. The person involved may not be the popular choice, but may be right for the task because he is committed to and capable of delivering the kind of results you need. Again, if you have the courage to appoint such a person, it will show the strength of your own commitment.

The converse is also true, in both cases. The kind of people you surround yourself with will speak volumes about you and the kind of future you envisage and the ways in which you think it can be attained.

Much has been spoken and written about the importance of team development. Less attention is paid to the importance of team selection. Stop mindless decisions about people and the jobs you want them to do. Make sure that your next choice sends a message throughout the church or organisation about your commitment to your top priority.

Learn to function effectively as a role model, and slowly but surely your team or church or organisation will start to come to life around the issue. Some of your efforts may be misdirected or useless—a few may even be harmful in the short term—but if you can sustain your endeavours, inevitably the organisation will shift its sights until it has them trained on your leadership vision.

KEY POINTS SUMMARY

Leadership is a symbolic activity and leaders need to lead in ways which send the right signals to their followers. This calls for 'appropriate' behaviour and is shown by the amount of time the leader spends on stated key issues and by the energy of his or her actions.

Leaders need to have clearly understood personal values which are reflected by their vision. They also need to discern the core values of their group and ensure that these are properly understood and that they express the right priorities. This requires consistent behaviour on the part of the leader.

There are at least three practical ways of ensuring that the right signals are sent and it is appropriate to send them in this way, provided they are in support of the right values.

Leaders need to exercise helpful behaviour while functioning as role models and this means assessing and fulfilling their responsibility to others and to themselves.

GUIDE FOR ACTION

Make an assessment of your personal values. Are any of them in conflict with your current, stated goals?

Discover the core values at work in your group. Use the list of questions given earlier in this chapter to assist you. How can these help you to exercise appropriate behaviour, consistent behaviour and helpful behaviour among your group?

Look at your current commitments. Change one day for the next five days so that your activities match your top priority.

Chapter Ten

EMPOWERING OTHERS TO ACHIEVE

But of a good leader, who talks little, When his work is done, his aim fulfilled, They will all say, 'We did this ourselves.'

Lao Tzu

Your position never gives you the right to command. It only imposes on you the duty of so living your life that others may receive your orders without being humiliated.

Dag Hammarskjold

It's not what you did that counts, it's what you got done.

Will Rogers

'Empowerment' is a buzz word. It means increasing the overall power of your team or organisation by increasing the power of the people who belong to it and work within it.

The church of Jesus Christ is an empowered organisation. Every member has the capacity to function in certain ways and the effectiveness of the church is increased as its individual members are enabled to fulfil their respective roles.

The analogy of a body is used to picture this way of working:

From him the whole body, joined and held together by every supporting ligament, grows and builds itself up in love, as each part does its work (Eph 4:16).

This holds good for Christian organisations and Christian groups and teams—right down to the smallest cell of operation.

However, this way of working requires that the principle of empowerment be firmly embedded in the process. People have to be informed, trained, supported and then released so that they can play their part to the full. The key to expanded results is to free individuals and organisations to act and to achieve. Empowerment rather than enslavement is a feature of effective leadership.

This implies that:

- Each member knows what his or her role or function is.
- They are committed to their roles.
- They are trained to perform their roles.
- They have all the support they need.

The picture is not one of independent action but of interaction and interdependence:

> **The eye cannot say to the hand, 'I don't need you!' And the head cannot say to the feet, 'I don't need you!' (1 Cor 12:21).**

The autonomy each member has is real and significant; there is full freedom of action allowing individual members to perform right up to the limit of their capability. But all this takes place in a context where there are controls which influence the timing and purpose of each action and which require co-ordination and co-operation with the actions of others.

Moses, arguably the greatest leader the people of Israel have ever had (Deut 34:11–12), learned the value of empowering others:

> **The next day Moses took his seat to serve as judge for the people, and they stood round him from morning till evening. When his father-in-law saw all that Moses was doing for the people, he said, 'What is this you are doing for the people? Why do you alone sit as judge, while all these people stand round you from morning till evening?'**

Moses answered him, 'Because the people come to me to seek God's will. Whenever they have a dispute, it is brought to me, and I decide between the parties and inform them of God's decrees and laws.'

Moses' father-in-law replied, 'What you are doing is not good. You and these people who come to you will only wear yourselves out. The work is too heavy for you; you cannot handle it alone. Listen now to me and I will give you some advice, and may God be with you. You must be the people's representative before God and bring their disputes to him. Teach them the decrees and laws, and show them the way to live and the duties they are to perform. But select capable men from all the people—men who fear God, trustworthy men who hate dishonest gain—and appoint them as officials over thousands, hundreds, fifties and tens. Have them serve as judges for the people at all times, but have them bring every difficult case to you; the simple cases they can decide themselves. That will make your load lighter, because they will share it with you. If you do this and God so commands, you will be able to stand the strain, and all these people will go home satisfied.'

Moses listened to his father-in-law and did everything he said (Exod 18:13–24).

This highlights an important development in the leadership of Israel. From it, four key messages emerge for leaders in relation to empowerment:

- Lead with vision, not tradition.
- Be an enabler, not a controller.
- Be a coach, not an expert.
- Be a link and a provider, not a hoarder.

Empowerment implies a new work contract between the leader and his or her followers. The shift towards this new way of working together is clearly shown by the arrangements Moses made following the advice he received from his concerned father-in-law. Four learning points emerge:

- Recognise what empowerment is.
- Realise when empowerment is needed.
- Create the context in which empowerment can take place.
- Make empowerment work.

Recognising what empowerment is

Churches and Christian organisations exist in an environment of rapid change. Beyond survival lies the more pressing need to be proactive and to respond positively to events in order to fulfil a God-given role. This means unlocking the full potential of those who people the organisation. This means enabling them to become:

- More self-reliant.
- More self-managing.
- More self-motivated.

This is exactly what happened in the case just described:

> **[Moses] chose capable men from all Israel and made them leaders of the people, officials over thousands, hundreds, fifties and tens. They served as judges for the people at all times. The difficult cases they brought to Moses, but the simple ones they decided themselves (Exod 18:25–26).**

Think about your own team. Jot down an activity or an area of work where you'd like them to show the three characteristics given above. Then note alongside each the benefits this might have for you!

SELF-RELIANCE   BENEFIT TO YOU

....

....

....

SELF-MANAGEMENT	BENEFIT TO YOU
....	....
....	....
....	....

SELF-MOTIVATION	BENEFIT TO YOU
....	....
....	....
....	....

From what you've written, ask yourself:

- Would the result be mutually beneficial?
- Would I be more empowered by my team's independence?
- Would the effect overall help to increase the power and productivity (fruitfulness!) of my team?

Empowerment leads to a radical rethink about what can be achieved in the future compared with what has been achieved in the past. There are jobs to be done, problems to be solved, decisions to be taken, plans to be made, arrangements to be put in hand, targets to be achieved, deadlines to be met. Empowerment is about transferring ownership of these, and the burden of responsibility that goes with them, to others.

This doesn't mean that the leader abdicates responsibility, opting for an easier life instead. In the case we've just considered, the role of Moses was undiminished; in fact his leadership effectiveness was enhanced as a result of the action he took.

Now, think about what you could do if you had more power. Tick the statements which apply to you.

If I had more power I'd be able to:

- Get things done quicker.
- Use more of my initiative.
- Make decisions and act accordingly.

- Be more adaptable to situations as they changed.
- Use more of my talents and abilities.
- Come up with more ideas.

Look at the statements you ticked. Now think about the members of your team. The same is probably true of them. So why not enable some of these things to happen by empowering them?

Realising when empowerment is needed

Moses' father-in-law, Jethro, quickly saw the need for empowerment in Moses' situation—not just in terms of benefits that would accrue, but also of problems that would be avoided. The people probably stood in long lines—apparently all day long—waiting to get a decision out of Moses. This is a pathetic scene and Jethro points to the inevitable outcome: the people, as well as the leader, are going to get worn out. The people become frustrated because of having to wait so long for results and the leader is worn out and exhausted from making all the decisions for the people and the organisation.

A similar scene can be witnessed in many churches and Christian organisations. People are worn out and fed up with waiting for something to happen as a result of their input or request, and the leadership is exhausted from trying to make all the right decisions itself.

Empowering others will help to achieve the following:

Make your job more manageable

Like Moses many modern Christian leaders are wearing themselves out trying to cope with the pressures and problems of running a Christian organisation. Empowerment of others will free you to concentrate on the more crucial aspects of your leadership responsibilities.

Increase the effectiveness of your organisation

You'll achieve more in less time and the results will be better.

Develop new leaders

Many Christian organisations lack strength in depth when it comes to leadership. This shortage of leaders keeps churches and organisations from growing as they should. Empowerment develops leadership ability. It gives people decision-making and problem-solving experience and helps to prepare them for greater responsibility by developing their skills. It also helps you to evaluate their potential.

Stimulate creativity

Empowerment makes people feel part of the team. It also increases their awareness of the importance of their individual role. This tends to make them look for ways of doing things better and of getting the kind of results that are needed.

Demonstrate trust and confidence in people's ability

What better way is there of showing this than by giving significant responsibility and holding the recipients accountable for results?

Leaders create either trust or distrust as the following diagrams show:

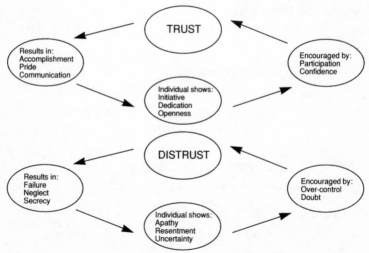

Creating the context in which empowerment can take place

'I'd rather put ten men to work,' said the great American evangelist, D. L. Moody, 'than do the work of ten men.'

Most would agree with him and there are many Christian and other leaders who happily hand over tasks and assign routine duties to their subordinates, almost as a matter of course, thinking that's all there is to it. But only rarely does the 'delegate' become empowered with real ownership and a real burden of responsibility. There is more to empowerment than simply 'putting people to work'.

There are four things you must do in order to create the kind of climate in which true empowerment can occur.

First, you must have a crystal clear vision about the ultimate goal towards which you are taking your church or organisation and you must ensure that those whom you are seeking to empower are in agreement with it—that is, that they believe in it as passionately as you do.

There is no real point in giving people jobs just to keep them occupied or to buy a little more time for yourself so that you can do the things you want to do. It is true that some activities will have value as learning and developmental experiences for certain people and this aspect should not be ignored (how else can the necessary experience be gained?). But if the arrangement is to have meaning other than that of a mechanical exercise, then it must be seen as one in which you are entrusting others with your vision, or part of it, and in which you are giving the responsibility for carrying it on to fulfilment. It goes without saying that if they don't see things the way you do then you are wasting your time.

The first rule of empowerment is to ensure that there is agreement about the vision. Suppose you are the minister of a church and your vision is to expand the church's activities and its service to the local community. To do this you recognise that it is necessary to acquire more land for building purposes and so on. Obtaining this land means engaging in hard negotiations with the authorities, bargaining over price and perhaps even offering certain concessions in return.

You have someone in your church who appears ideally suited to do this on your behalf. He has the right blend of skills and experience. He knows who to contact. There's only one snag: this person doesn't really believe that the church ought to be buying more land at this time. He doesn't share your vision, although he hasn't openly said so.

To send such a person to negotiate on the church's behalf would probably be a waste of time. You may believe that by empowering him to act in this way, you have done enough. You have not; the climate is wrong. You either need to convince him about the vision or send someone else. In fact you'd do better sending another, who believes as you do, even though he or she has less experience and fewer contacts. For one thing, the second person won't take 'no' for an answer; the first one probably will. The second person will drive on until he or she gets a result. The first will give up the quest at an early stage and may even be relieved to report back to you that there's nothing doing.

The second thing you have to do is set extremely high standards which you live, transmit and demand from others. Clarify your expectations; let people know what is acceptable and what is not. Communicate essential information, results needed, timescales involved. Communicate attitudes, behavioural norms, performance criteria. Empowering others does not mean that you relinquish control. A shared vision represents a paperless form of control; setting standards creates account-ability and this is one of the most powerful forms of control available. Letting people know how performance will be assessed and how results will be evaluated leaves them free to operate in their own way within the boundaries you set.

Thirdly, you must show that you believe in the people you are empowering. This means letting go of the reins and not taking them back. It means giving them authority and letting them use it. The people Moses entrusted with the task of judging his people had no experience of this kind of work. Their CVs, had they possessed them, would have shown most of them to be bricklayers and labourers! But he believed in them wholeheartedly. This faith in people is key and you can show it in the following ways:

(a) Provide back-up for their decisions. You don't have to agree with them at all times, but you must never leave them to twist slowly in the wind. Your people depend on you. If you don't back them up when they need you, their trust in you will be undermined.

(b) Don't focus on mistakes. Mistakes speak loudly; success is often quiet. Once people realise they've made errors, leave it. Don't rub it in. Emphasise the positive. Focus on efforts, not circumstances.

(c) Don't spy on people. There is a fine line to be drawn between spying and simply checking up on something. Where possible, check directly with the person concerned.

(d) Don't withhold information as a test. Practise openness. Be open with information and with your feelings. Don't keep people guessing.

(e) Show respect and exercise simple courtesy. Say 'please' and 'thank-you', phrase orders in the form of requests and don't lean on the prerogatives of your position. Don't make them wait unnecessarily for a hearing. Don't needlessly interrupt and don't pull rank to gratify your own ego.

(f) Don't manipulate. Be honest and keep the information flowing.

Finally, you need to keep in touch with those you have empowered to ensure that they have all the support they need. Let them bite off more than they can chew if they insist, but make sure they don't choke.

Sometimes you can make the mistake of thinking that it's best not to make contact with people while they're doing the work; that you should keep out of the way and let them get on with it. But it is good policy to maintain communication with them—not in order to interfere or impose on them, but to let them know you're there to give advice if needed, and to let them see that you are interested.

Making empowerment work

Having created a climate which ensures that empowerment can work, the next step is to make it work.

There are three key words which define the process:

- Responsibility
- Authority
- Accountability

Empowerment is the process of transferring responsibility, authority and accountability from one person or group to another.

Responsibility

This has to be defined precisely in relation to the role and task requirements. The case study described in Exodus 18 makes clear what the responsibilities of the newly-appointed judges were to be.

Authority

This has to be given unequivocally. It is apparent from the same biblical record that the authority given to the judges was absolute, within certain prescribed limits. It was given in relation to certain groups of people and it was to be exercised in dealing with cases described as 'simple'. This authority was sufficient to allow them to fulfil their appointed role. Imagine, by way of comparison, a group of deacons in a local church who have responsibility for running a cost-effective buildings maintenance programme, but who have no authority to spend money! They are not an empowered group and will soon become frustrated with their task.

Accountability

People have to be made accountable by defining standards of performance and specifying the kind of results which are required. This leaves them free to work in their own way and gives scope for initiative.

Having effected the transfer, the greatest test of empowerment is for the leader to let go! The temptation is to take back the reins after a while. Here are some points to ponder:

- Have you communicated the vision with clarity? Is it obvious that your people are committed to it?
- Have you shown in the past that you trust your people's judgement?
- Have you given people enough authority to ensure that they don't have to come running to you at frequent intervals?
- Do the standards you have set make plain the level of performance you expect?
- Have you made it clear by your total inaction that you are not going to jump in as a critical deadline approaches and start asking lots of questions which show your worries about the situation? For example, 'They need that article for publication on Friday. Is it going to be ready?' (It's only Monday and your team have the matter perfectly well in hand.)

The empowering leader works with his team and does not overpower them in order to control what is happening. Here are some examples:

Decision-making

In many organisations, decisions are made at the top and passed down. Try instead to focus decision-making at the point of most relevant experience and expertise, that is, enabling decisions to be made by those who'll carry out the work.

Think back to the last decision you made alone. What advantages and disadvantages would there have been if this had been made participatively? Write them down:

ADVANTAGES   DRAWBACKS

....

....

....

Letting people make decisions about their work goes a long way towards ensuring that they'll 'own' the decision and be sufficiently motivated to see the work carried out to a high standard. As an empowering leader you may need to give them guidelines about managing the decision-making process. This is a matter of coaching people to ensure that they are competent to deal with their responsibilities.

Informing

If people are to be empowered they need information.

Jot down the last item of important information you shared with a member of your team.

....

....

Now write down what extra information you could have given them on the same topic—perhaps some more detail or additional information that would have put the task into wider perspective.

....

....

Identify what type of information you don't currently give your team but which you'll try to provide in future.

....

....

Planning

As an empowering leader try to involve people whose inputs and interest would be useful. Work together to:

- Set priorities.
- Schedule activities.
- Set tasks.

When people are involved in agreeing goals they tend to set higher targets for themselves.

Developing

As people become empowered they need new skills and knowledge. As an empowering leader you must constantly look for ways of developing people through training and other kinds of learning experience. You have a twin role as:

- Coach: enabling people to improve their competence.
- Mentor: taking an interest in their progress.

Make a note of three knowledge and/or skill items your team will need to acquire as your empowerment strategy takes hold.

....

....

Here are some additional things you can do to support your people on the path to empowerment:

- Ensure your help is available and forthcoming.
- Listen to people and get to know them better.
- Verbalise key issues clearly.
- Be direct and honest.

Lastly, get into the habit of examining every act of delegation regularly. Have you really snipped all the strings necessary to transfer 'ownership'? Examine the context closely. Is there real agreement about the vision? Are your standards known to be high?

Empowerment is a fascinating concept. We must come to terms with it and with its implications, preferably sooner rather than later.

KEY POINTS SUMMARY

Empowerment is about giving other people 'ownership' of the task. It involves a transfer of responsibility, authority and accountability from you to them.

Exodus 18:13–26 offers a good case study about empowerment, outlining why it is needed and how it works.

A certain kind of context has to be established first before a policy of empowerment can be made to work. The requirements are for a shared vision, high standards which are known, faith in people and the capacity to stay in touch as coach and mentor.

For the process of empowerment to work the leader has to be prepared to let go in a total sense.

The benefits of empowerment outweigh the risks. The challenge facing leaders is one of mastering the art and then of being bold enough to implement the process.

GUIDE FOR ACTION

Imagine you are going to explain to someone about your intentions as an empowering leader. Write down short descriptions of what you are trying to achieve:

Why I'm empowering this team (or individual)

....

....

....

What I think it will achieve

....

....

....

How I'll go about it

....

....

....

PART FOUR
Successful Leadership Strategies

The leader has the task of creating a true whole that is larger than the sum of its parts, a productive entity that turns out to be more than the sum of the resources put into it. One analogy is the conductor of the Symphony Orchestra, through whose effort, vision and leadership individual instrumental parts that are so much noise by themselves, become the living whole of the music. But the conductor has the composer's score; he is only the interpreter. The leader is both composer and conductor.

Peter F. Drucker, The Practice of Management

Chapter Eleven

KEY QUESTIONS TO ASK

This final section provides a basis for reviewing the key messages of the book and also for developing agendas which will help you as a leader to establish personal action plans for bringing about improvements in specific areas of knowledge, skill and strategy where you have identified a need.

This chapter creates an initial focus for you by leading you to consider a number of *key questions* relating to the way in which you practise leadership.

These deal with:

- The leadership role.
- Personal values.
- Vision and goals.
- Leadership influence.
- Leadership agendas.

Each question is treated separately and covers:

- The broad implications for leadership.
- Key considerations.
- Steps to take (references to the main text are included).

What is my precise leadership role?

This is perhaps the most fundamental question any leader, or prospective leader, could ask. Certain things are implied. The first is that you are prepared to accept the challenge of leadership. Do you recall the words of President Truman? 'If you can't stand the heat then stay out of the kitchen!' Have you ever wondered why there are more followers than leaders? One reason is because it's easier to follow than to lead.

A second inference is that you understand what leadership involves. As you endeavour to clarify your role, you'll find it useful to look again at Chapter Three of this book.

Again, you might ask yourself, 'Why do I want to be a leader?' This has an important bearing on the main question we're addressing right now. Set your thoughts down here:

....

....

....

....

....

....

....

....

Are you satisfied with what you've written?

Below is a simple table. It lists different facets of the leadership role. Think about them in relation to your own leadership situation, then rank them in order of importance to you. For example, if you think that point 9 is the most important, then put 1 in the 'order of importance' column. Exclude any items which don't relate to your role. (There are two more columns headed 'least difficult' and 'most difficult'. Ignore these for the moment.)

MY LEADERSHIP ROLE

	Role	Order of importance	Least difficult	Most difficult
1	Group leader: directly responsible for leading a group.			
2	Liaison: communicating with other groups on behalf of your own.			
3	Information sharing: giving information to your group and to the church or organisation.			
4	Information seeking: getting information from your group and from other sections of the church or organisation.			
5	Spokesman: representing the group, church or organisation to the outside world.			
6	Innovator: developing and facilitating the development of new ideas.			
7	Empowerment: deciding what individuals within the group, church or organisation should do.			
8	Disturbance handler: coping with conflicts and discipline issues.			
9	Negotiator: bargaining with people inside and outside your sphere of control.			
10	Performance appraiser: assessing individual performance.			
11	Trainer: developing people's skills.			

The same table has been completed by a significant number of Christian leaders across the United Kingdom, among them being ministers of churches, youth leaders, house-group leaders, Sunday school superintendents, evangelists and leaders in Christian organisations. Look at the next table and compare your ratings with theirs.

MY LEADERSHIP ROLE

	Role	Order of importance	Least difficult	Most difficult
1	Group leader: directly responsible for leading a group.	1		
2	Liaison: communicating with other groups on behalf of your own.	8		
3	Information sharing: giving information to your group and to the church or organisation.	4		
4	Information seeking: getting information from your group and from other sections of the church or organisation.	7		
5	Spokesman: representing the group, church or organisation to the outside world.	10		
6	Innovator: developing and facilitating the development of new ideas.	2		
7	Empowerment: deciding what individuals within the group, church or organisation should do.	3		
8	Disturbance handler: coping with conflicts and discipline issues.	6		
9	Negotiator: bargaining with people inside and outside your sphere of control.	11		
10	Performance appraiser: assessing individual performance.	9		
11	Trainer: developing people's skills.	5		

This exercise should help you to start thinking in a fairly structured way about your particular role as a leader, especially in the context of how other Christian leaders see theirs.

Which of the following words would you use to describe your role (underline three only)?

- Pioneer
- Carer
- Guardian
- Guide
- Co-ordinator
- Inspirer
- Encourager
- Builder
- Caretaker
- Cultivator

Am I clear about my personal values and are they sound?

There are two issues which may confront you as a leader in relation to the values you possess. The first is a matter of knowing what your values are—you may have to clarify them. The second is in being sure that your values are correct—you may have to change them.

Chapter One introduces the question of the leader and his values. The topic is dealt with again, in more depth, in Chapter Nine.

Here are some characteristics of leaders with clear/unclear values:

CLEAR	UNCLEAR
Frequently questions own values.	Fails to question own values.
Changes values in the light of evidence.	Ignores evidence that conflicts with values.
Tends to be consistent.	Tends to be inconsistent.
Behaves in line with stated values.	Behaves differently from stated values.
Exposes own viewpoints for comment.	Does not expose own viewpoints.
Takes firm stand.	Unwilling to take firm stand.
Seeks feedback on own approach.	Avoids feedback.

Clarifying your values

The process of clarifying values can be achieved systematically by working through the following steps:

Decide to be truthful: Values are only revealed when an issue is being considered. Be prepared to express your views fully, even though you may dislike what you are saying or feeling, or find that some of your views are inconsistent. You have to find out where you stand at present.

Review alternatives: Explore the issues and examine other viewpoints. Identifying other value choices is a first step. Test how you react to these alternatives and decide which are your values. A fully explored value is one which has been identified and freely chosen from other well-explored alternatives.

Test for consistency: As values are clarified, inconsistencies may appear in your total value system. This is a cue to re-examine those issues in more depth. Values need to be realistically evaluated, even if they challenge your concept of how you should behave.

Check against behaviour: It often happens that individuals determine their values and then proceed to ignore them in practice. This can occur because people express views they feel they ought to hold rather than those to which they are genuinely committed. Behaving contrary to expressed values may be a sign that you're not fully committed to the value judgements you have made. This is especially relevant where spiritual and moral issues are involved; it is not sufficient to quote Scripture and claim, 'These are my values.' You may need to do some more work.

Group values

Leaders do not work in isolation. They are influenced partly by the values which prevail within the church, organisation or group to which they belong. Sometimes this can present problems. The alignment of corporate and personal values can vary from support to disagreement as follows:

Fully supportive: Your energy goes towards supporting the church, organisation or group stance.

Acceptance: You understand and have no real difficulty supporting the corporate view.

Toleration: Despite definite differences, you can live with the situation. You may even be able to influence matters to make the other approach more compatible with your own.

Profound disagreement: The most difficult position. Your options include grudging acceptance, sabotage, ignoring the other view, attempting to influence it or withdrawal.

You must take active steps to clarify the corporate view, and also your stance in relation to it. Remember, clarification may lead to the need for change on your part.

Am I clear about my vision and goals?

Chapter Seven and Chapter Eight deal with these topics.

By definition almost, leaders are taking people and things in a certain direction. They are challenging the status quo and are moving towards a goal. As a leader, are you crystal clear about where you are going? About what you are desirous of achieving? If you have no vision at present, are you engaged in the process of acquiring one and of developing it into a form suitable for communicating to others?

If you have no vision to present, it is arguable that you will never get off first base as a leader. Your leadership influence will atrophy.

Your vision should:

- Be different.
- Be inspiring.
- Make sense.
- Be relevant.
- Be God-given and God-centred.

Goals are something else. They are the milestones on the way to full attainment of the desired vision. They need definition and they should be specific, measurable and attainable. Here is a simple algorithm for you to follow; it may help you to arrive at some answers:

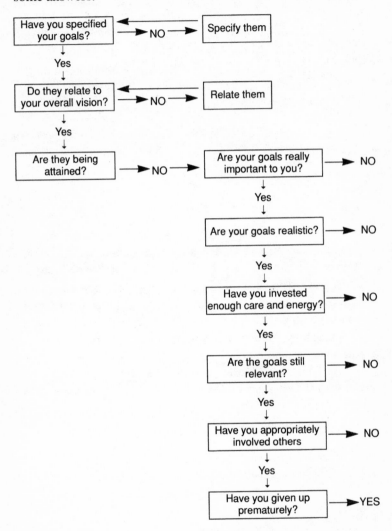

Do I need to increase my leadership influence?

Leaders exert influence on people and situations. That is how they make things happen. When this is taking place it will be seen that they are using their authority in certain ways. All leaders have some kind of authority; without it they are powerless to lead. What kind of authority do you think you have? Look back to Chapter Four. Are you using your authority in the most appropriate ways and to the best advantage?

Do you have a particular leadership style?

Is it right for the situation you find yourself in and for the people you are trying to lead?

Are you satisfied with your influencing skills? To help you decide, here is a list of things which characterise leaders whose influence is low:

- Feel undervalued.
- Have little impact on others.
- Are ignorant of the influence process.
- Dress inappropriately.
- Have weak physical stance.
- Lack assertion.
- Are aggressive.
- Make poor personal contact.
- Fail to reward others.
- Give unclear directions.
- Have no strategy for influencing groups.

The answers to the following questions could show what is stopping you from exerting influence.

- Who do you influence most?
- Who would you like to influence?
- What is your strategy for influencing others?
- Who influences you?
- When do you feel ineffective?
- When do you feel powerful?

Am I pursuing the right things as a leader?

What kind of items do you have on your leadership agenda? Think first about your own personal development (see Chapter Two).

Turn back to the 'My Leadership Role' table you completed earlier in this chapter and fill in the columns headed 'least difficult' and 'most difficult'. Consider each role in relation to the difficulty you have in fulfilling it. Tick the two you have least difficulty with; then tick the two with which you have most difficulty. You may find it useful to compare your results with those of other Christian leaders sampled using the same table.

Role	% said 'least difficult'	% said 'most difficult'
Group leader	18	10
Liaison	5	3
Information sharing	18	0
Information seeking	13	3
Spokesman	8	5
Innovator	8	8
Empowerer	16	8
Disturbance handler	3	21
Negotiator	8	5
Performance appraiser	0	21
Trainer	3	16

Think about the two roles with which you experience least difficulty. Under the headings of Knowledge, Skills and Setting list the factors which help you perform those roles.

Least difficult	First role	Second role
Knowledge (what you need to know)		
Skill (what you need to be able to do)		
Setting (attitudes of others; extent to which roles are defined, etc.)		

Next, think about the two roles with which you experience most difficulty. Under the same headings of Knowledge, Skills and Setting list the factors which contribute to your difficulty.

Most difficult	First role	Second role
Knowledge (what you need to know)		
Skill (what you need to be able to do)		
Setting (attitudes of others; extent to which roles are defined, etc.)		

This exercise will help you to identify a number of key issues relating to your personal development.

Another item on your leadership agenda might be organisational development. Are there any adaptations or changes you need to make? Here are a few things you might consider:

- Adding new members to the team.
- Clarifying or changing the organisation structure.
- Developing teamwork.

Finally, give some thought to your leadership strategies. Using jargon we could say that strategies are concerned with transforming 'inputs' into 'outputs'. The idea can be shown in diagram form, like this:

An 'output' is a desired result, for example, to communicate a vision; to attain a goal associated with it; to develop individuals; to build teams; to change an organisation structure or to solve a problem.

An 'input' is the application of whatever is needed to achieve the output, for example, skills, money, effort, information or resources. 'Transformation' is the process by which inputs are changed to outputs.

For instance, if you wanted to establish a branch of your church on a nearby local housing estate (desired output), what inputs would you need? Try listing a few:

....

....

Now, what is the best way of using those inputs to obtain the outcome you are seeking (transformation)?

This prompts three questions for leaders as they develop their strategies:

- What outputs are required?
- What is the best way to transform inputs?
- What inputs are needed to make the process happen?

This chapter does not set out to provide answers; its main aim is to prompt you into asking the right questions. There is nothing quite as useless as the right answer to-the wrong question! Asking questions that are pertinent to your leadership circumstances will lead you towards finding answers that are right for you.

Chapter Twelve

ACTION PLANS TO DEVELOP

This chapter continues the process of review and application by focusing attention on major leadership tasks and showing how practical agendas for action can be developed.

Areas covered are:

- Creating the vision.
- Implementing change.
- Developing the organisation.
- Improving team effectiveness.

Creating the vision

A total of seven criteria have been identified in relation to this activity. Consider the statements against each of the seven and circle the letter against the one which best describes your organisation, church or group at present, ie, either A, B or C. Complete the profile at the end of the section. From this you will see where you need to take action to get you from where you perceive yourself to be in relation to creating a vision to where you want to be.

To help you relate to the criteria imagine that you are the leader of a small, struggling, inner-city church. The building you occupy is badly in need of repair. Funds are low and attendances are dwindling, but you are determined to carry on, somehow. . .

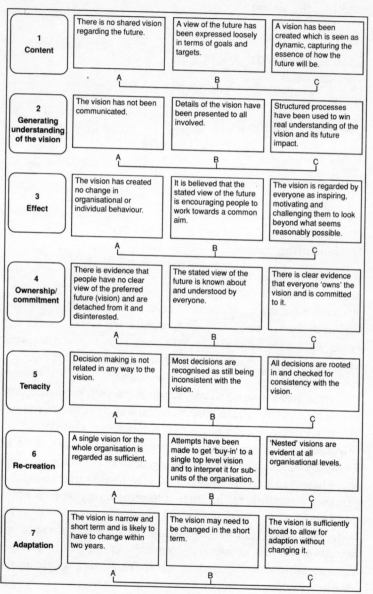

	A	B	C
1 **Content**	There is no shared vision regarding the future.	A view of the future has been expressed loosely in terms of goals and targets.	A vision has been created which is seen as dynamic, capturing the essence of how the future will be.
2 **Generating understanding of the vision**	The vision has not been communicated.	Details of the vision have been presented to all involved.	Structured processes have been used to win real understanding of the vision and its future impact.
3 **Effect**	The vision has created no change in organisational or individual behaviour.	It is believed that the stated view of the future is encouraging people to work towards a common aim.	The vision is regarded by everyone as inspiring, motivating and challenging them to look beyond what seems reasonably possible.
4 **Ownership/ commitment**	There is evidence that people have no clear view of the preferred future (vision) and are detached from it and disinterested.	The stated view of the future is known about and understood by everyone.	There is clear evidence that everyone 'owns' the vision and is committed to it.
5 **Tenacity**	Decision making is not related in any way to the vision.	Most decisions are recognised as still being inconsistent with the vision.	All decisions are rooted in and checked for consistency with the vision.
6 **Re-creation**	A single vision for the whole organisation is regarded as sufficient.	Attempts have been made to get 'buy-in' to a single top level vision and to interpret it for sub-units of the organisation.	'Nested' visions are evident at all organisational levels.
7 **Adaptation**	The vision is narrow and short term and is likely to have to change within two years.	The vision may need to be changed in the short term.	The vision is sufficiently broad to allow for adaption without changing it.

PROFILE

Creating the vision

	A	B	C
Content			
Generating understanding of the vision			
Effect			
Ownership/commitment			
Tenacity			
Re-Creation			
Adaptation			

Implementing change

A total of eight criteria have been identified in relation to this activity under the sub-headings of: 'Preparing an Action Plan', 'Introducing the Change' and 'Implementing the Action Plan'. Consider the statements against each of the eight criteria and circle the letter against the one which best describes your organisation, church or group at present, ie, either A, B or C.

Complete the profile at the end of the section. From this you will see where you need to take action to get you from where you perceive yourself to be in relation to the way you currently tackle the job of implementing change, to where you want to be.

To help you relate the criteria to a real-life situation, think of how they might apply in the following circumstances: You are the manager of a medium-sized Christian bookshop. You want to extend the ministry of the shop by turning a section of it into a coffee area. This means that some of the staff, all of whom are volunteers, will have to serve in the coffee area instead of the bookshop. No one knows about your vision except the management committee to whom you report. They have approved the idea in principle. Now it's over to you to introduce it...

PREPARING AN ACTION PLAN

1 **Process**	No method has been established for developing an action plan.	A team has been set up to develop an action plan and is evolving its own way of achieving this task.	The action plan has been developed by a representative team using a structured approach.
	A	B	C
2 **Progressive milestones**	No milestones have been identified to enable measurement of progress with the plan.	Milestones have been identified, but they have not been communicated outside the planning team.	The plan includes milestones for the regular assessment of progress and these are publicly known.
	A	B	C
3 **Resource availability**	Resources needed to implement the action plan have not been specified.	Resources needed have been specified and scheduled.	Resources needed have been accurately specified, their availability checked and guaranteed.
	A	B	C

INTRODUCING THE CHANGE

4 **Responsibility for change**	It is not clear who is responsible for the various aspects of the change programme.	People responsible for managing each aspect of the programme know what is expected and how the changes are to be achieved.	People responsible for specific aspects of the change programme are fully prepared to fulfil the role and are providing the leadership and motivation needed to achieve the objectives.
	A	B	C
5 **Communicating the need for change**	Communicating the 'why', 'what' and 'how' of the change to everyone affected has not been thought through or tackled systematically.	People are informed of planned changes and of the reasons and likely impact of same.	Everyone involved in the change has the opportunity to discuss these and make suggestions on how best to achieve the results envisaged.
	A	B	C
6 **Consequences for individuals**	Little thought is given to the impact of proposed changes on individuals.	Individuals affected by the changes are informed of the impact this will have on them.	The impact of change is discussed with individuals, and their concerns, if any, are registered. Efforts are made to respond positively to these concerns and needs.
	A	B	C

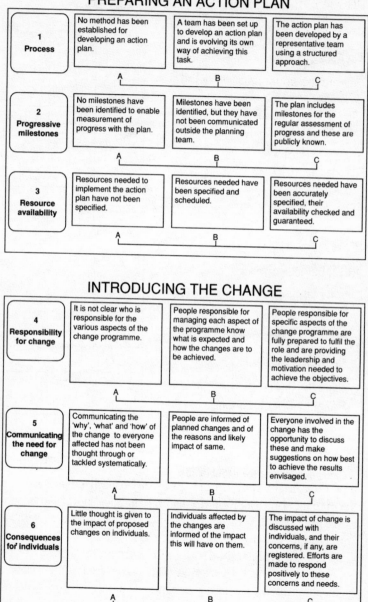

IMPLEMENTING THE ACTION PLAN

7 Review mechanisms	There is little emphasis put on regularly reviewing changes sought.	Mechanisms exist for reviewing each part of the change programme.	All aspects of the change programme are regularly reviewed by those responsible for implementing it and those affected by it.
	A	B	C

8 Corrective action	Once set in motion change activities are implemented but don't always meet set objectives.	Any corrective action is decided by the person leading the change activity.	Where the desired progress has not been achieved, corrective action is taken by the person leading that activity and by those involved with it, so that objectives are attained.
	A	B	C

PROFILE

Implementing change

	A	B	C
Action planning: Process			
Progress milestones			
Resource availability			
Introducing the change: Responsibility for change			
Communicating the need for change			
Consequences for individuals			
Implementing the action plan: Review mechanisms			
Corrective action			

Developing the organisation

This covers two aspects: (a) defining organisational needs and (b) strategies for developing the organisation to enable it to cope with problems and take advantage of opportunities.

A total of eight criteria have been identified in relation to this activity under the sub-headings of: 'Defining organisational needs' and 'Organisational development strategy'. Consider the statements against each of the eight criteria and circle the letter against the one which best describes your organisation, church or group at present, ie, either A, B or C. Complete the profile at the end of the section. From this you will see where you need to take action to get you from where you perceive yourself to be to where you want to be.

To help you relate to circumstances in which these criteria can be a useful guide in developing the right strategies, turn back to Chapter Ten. Consider the case study involving Moses and the judging of his people. Imagine you are Jethro and you can see that your son-in-law needs help. The organisation he controls isn't up to the job it has to do; it needs to be altered so that it can cope with the emerging problems and opportunities it faces. How will you advise him? Ponder the criteria before you decide what to say.

DEFINING ORGANISATIONAL NEEDS

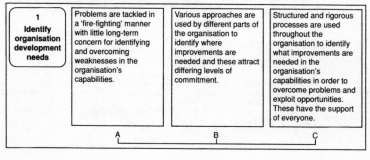

1 Identify organisation development needs	Problems are tackled in a 'fire-fighting' manner with little long-term concern for identifying and overcoming weaknesses in the organisation's capabilities.	Various approaches are used by different parts of the organisation to identify where improvements are needed and these attract differing levels of commitment.	Structured and rigorous processes are used throughout the organisation to identify what improvements are needed in the organisation's capabilities in order to overcome problems and exploit opportunities. These have the support of everyone.
	A	B	C

2 **Framework**	There is no framework against which problems and opportunities can be explored.	There is a stated vision framework against which problems/opportunities can be explored, and which would enable solutions to be evaluated.	There is a stated vision against which problems/ opportunities are explored and solutions found beyond what would normally seem possible.
	A	B	C
3 **Responsibility**	Responsibility for solving problems and exploiting opportunities is not clearly defined, nor is the commitment to doing so readily visible.	Responsibility for solving problems and exploiting opportunities is defined, but commitment to doing so is not visible.	Responsibility for tackling problems/opportunities is clearly defined and there is evidence that those responsible 'own' the task and are committed to it.
	A	B	C

ORGANISATIONAL DEVELOPMENT STRATEGY

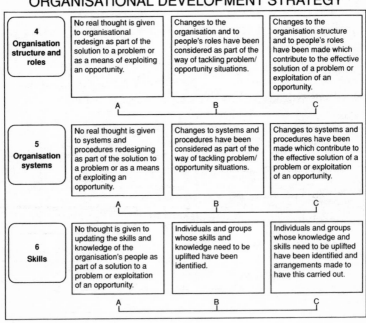

4 **Organisation structure and roles**	No real thought is given to organisational redesign as part of the solution to a problem or as a means of exploiting an opportunity.	Changes to the organisation and to people's roles have been considered as part of the way of tackling problem/ opportunity situations.	Changes to the organisation structure and to people's roles have been made which contribute to the effective solution of a problem or exploitation of an opportunity.
	A	B	C
5 **Organisation systems**	No real thought is given to systems and procedures redesigning as part of the solution to a problem or as a means of exploiting an opportunity.	Changes to systems and procedures have been considered as part of the way of tackling problem/ opportunity situations.	Changes to systems and procedures have been made which contribute to the effective solution of a problem or exploitation of an opportunity.
	A	B	C
6 **Skills**	No thought is given to updating the skills and knowledge of the organisation's people as part of a solution to a problem or exploitation of an opportunity.	Individuals and groups whose skills and knowledge need to be uplifted have been identified.	Individuals and groups whose knowledge and skills need to be uplifted have been identified and arrangements made to have this carried out.
	A	B	C

7 Relationships/ communication	Little thought is given to the need to make changes in working relationships and communication processes as part of the way of tackling problems/opportunities.	New forms of relationships and communication processes between groups have been explored but not specified.	Revised forms of working relationships and communications have been specified and actions agreed upon.
	A	B	C

8 Leadership style	Little thought is given to modifying leadership style as a means of solving problems/ exploiting opportunities.	The need to modify leadership style has been explored and some broad changes specified.	Modifications to leadership style necessary to underpin changes in strategy and structure etc. have been defined and actions agreed upon.
	A	B	C

PROFILE

Developing the organisation

	A	B	C
Defining organisational needs: Identifying organisational needs			
Framework			
Responsibility			
Organisational development strategy: Organisation structure and roles			
Organisation systems			
Skills			
Relationships/communication			
Leadership style			

Improving team effectiveness

Five different kinds of team are described in Chapter Three. Effective teams are characterised by the following:

Common purpose	Everybody understands and is working towards the same end.
Clear roles and responsibilities	Members know what their contribution to the team is and what every other member is responsible for doing.
Effective procedures	The team has sound procedures for making decisions and carrying out agreed actions. The right people are involved and the necessary information is available. Methods of implementing decisions are understood, and everybody is committed to making them work.
Supporting relationships	Team members support each other and develop interpersonal relationships based on trust and co-operation. Members are open with each other and handle conflict constructively.
Two-way communication	The team leader communicates and listens. Team members provide ideas and all have the opportunity to put forward their views.
Effective use of team members	The team has the range of individual skills to achieve its task and uses the skills fully for the benefit of the team. The team plays to its strengths and develops talent.
Learning from mistakes	Members are encouraged to review their performance and receive feedback on it.
Standards of performance	Members are encouraged to achieve. Standards are developed through commitment.

| Responsiveness to change | Information is shared. Individuals are involved, and their concerns are taken into account. |
| Inter-group relationship characteristics | These are sound and are based on the foregoing. |

With these characteristics in mind, complete the following questionnaire on team effectiveness. You can do this by yourself and, if you think it appropriate, you could get the members of your group of co-workers to complete it also.

The questionnaire consists of a series of ten sets of statements which you or your fellow workers might make about teamwork in your group. For each set you should allocate a total of ten points between the statements that appear broadly correct with regard to your group. Points may be allocated to just one statement or spread as you wish. Don't spend a lot of time on each statement—your first reaction should be enough. Write the points you allocate in the appropriate box on the answer grid which is provided at the end of the questionnaire. When you have finished, count up the number of points you have scored in each vertical column, ie, how many in the 'A' column, how many in the 'B' column and so on. Write this total in the box provided at the bottom of each column.

1. A No one is really clear about where we are going.
    B Individuals are not clearly accountable for their actions.
    C The leader rarely asks for the opinion of team members.
    D Members could contribute more than they are asked to.
    E We punish failure.
    F We rarely change the way we do things.
    G We are often in conflict with other groups.
    H We often let our operating standards slip.
    I Differences between team members are taken personally.
    J Decisions are taken at the wrong level.

2. A We are always busy but never seem to get anywhere.
   B Members don't know what is expected of them.
   C Members don't get the chance to put forward ideas.
   D The leader doesn't use his team according to its strengths.
   E Members are prone to covering up their mistakes.
   F The team is unwilling to change.
   G Relationships with other groups are cool.
   H The team's operating performance is variable.
   I Members don't expect support from their colleagues.
   J The leader doesn't involve the right people in making decisions.

3. A The leader and team don't spend enough time planning ahead.
   B Members seem to duplicate each other's efforts.
   C Members are not kept up to date.
   D Little effort is made to develop people.
   E Serious operating errors should be a matter for discipline.
   F We rarely look for ways to improve.
   G We rarely work well with other teams.
   H Our performance is worse than that of other teams doing similar work.
   I We are not open with each other about our work issues.
   J We don't have the information to make good decisions.

4. A Members do not have a clear view of what is expected of them.
   B Individual responsibilities are not clear.
   C There are often complaints about poor communication.
   D Not enough use is made of the talent there is within the team.
   E We do not discuss why something went wrong.
   F Suggestions for improvement are not welcomed.
   G Other parts of the organisation are little help to us.

H   Operating standards vary according to who is doing the work.

I   Members tend to be defensive about their individual responsibilities.

J   Unpopular decisions are not implemented.

5. A   Priorities are unclear.

B   People do not know what their place is in the team.

C   Members don't know what developments are planned within their department.

D   We are not aware of the skills group members have.

E   Suggestions for improvement are not encouraged.

F   We do things well enough as it is.

G   Other groups don't understand what it is we're trying to do.

H   We do not have clear operating standards.

I   It's fair game to ridicule colleagues.

J   The team is not sufficiently involved in decision making.

6. A   The team doesn't know what other groups in other parts of the organisation are aiming for.

B   Poor organisation is the cause of some failures.

C   The leader doesn't make a point of updating his team.

D   We don't define the skills we need in our team.

E   Feedback from other groups is not welcome.

F   We resist pressure to change from those we serve.

G   We spend lots of time justifying our needs to other groups.

H   It doesn't matter how we do it as long as we're the best.

I   We tend to take advantage of each other's weaknesses.

J   We make decisions but nothing seems to happen.

7. A   We don't discuss developments with our 'customers' and 'suppliers'.

B   It isn't always clear who should be taking decisions.

C   Members don't get much chance to talk to the leader.

D   Some team members have relevant skills which are not used.

E   We don't learn from our failures.
F   Things have changed too much already.
G   Other groups don't give us the support we need.
H   We don't set ourselves high standards of performance.
I   People won't say what they really mean.
J   Individual members don't know who is making some of the decisions.

8. A   Within the organisation, different groups are pulling in different directions.
    B   Things don't get done unless someone is specifically given the job.
    C   The leader rarely listens to individual team members.
    D   We don't consider ability when a job needs to be done.
    E   Members don't receive feedback on their performance.
    F   Ideas are rejected if they are going to cause disruption.
    G   We make too many operating errors.
    H   Our operating standards are high because we drive people hard.
    I   We don't take time to resolve differences between us.
    J   Decisions seem to be made behind closed doors.

9. A   We concentrate only on achieving results.
    B   Members don't know the limits of their authority.
    C   Some team members would never get a fair hearing.
    D   I could make better use of the skills of my people.
    E   We don't spend enough time questioning the things we do.
    F   People here don't understand the need for change.
    G   Information does not flow freely between teams.
    H   It's every man for himself in this team.
    I   People don't implement the decisions they disagree with.

10. A   We seem to be reacting to events all the time.
    B   We argue about whose responsibility some jobs are.
    C   The team often feels it is working in the dark.

D We are not good at getting the best out of people.
E We spend too much time doing and not enough time thinking.
F We don't look outside for good ideas.
G A lot of effort goes into resolving conflict with other groups.
H Our operating standards are not demanding.
I   We don't really share skills and information as a team.
J   People often don't know that a decision has been made.

TEAM EFFECTIVENESS QUESTIONNAIRE
ANSWER GRID

QUESTION	STATEMENT									
	A	B	C	D	E	F	G	H	I	J
1										
2										
3										
4										
5										
6										
7										
8										
9										
10										
TOTALS										

Add up the scores in each column and put the results in the appropriate TOTAL box.

The questionnaire is based on the ten characteristics of effective teamwork. The Summary Profile which follows relates each column of the grid to its characteristic.

A   Common purpose.

B   Clear roles and responsibilities.

C   Regular two-way communication.

D   Effective use of team members.

E   Learning from mistakes.

F   Responsiveness to change.

G   Sound inter-group relations.

H   Standards of performance.

I   Supporting relationships.

J   Effective procedures.

What do the results mean? Simply that those columns with the highest totals indicate the characteristics which represent your team's greatest areas of weakness. Of course these results are fairly subjective and you should bear this in mind as you attempt to make use of them.

Where do you go from here? It's really up to you. Having pinpointed areas of weakness in your teamwork you now need to come up with an action plan to deal with them.

This chapter contains only a general framework for analysis and review, but it should allow you to construct your own agendas for action.

Chapter Thirteen

EXAMPLES TO FOLLOW

Any attempt to summarise the convictions and practices of leaders who succeed at the task is bound to be incomplete. However, the following things seem to be held in common.

Common traits of successful leaders

Force of personality

This stems from well-integrated, powerful convictions. They appear to have an anchor point that keeps them stable, even calm, in times of stress and difficulty. They are not easily driven off course because they have an inner compass that points the way for them.

Realism

They have the capacity to search out reality and face it honestly, even humbly. Truth and facts become the basis and standard for their actions. People recognise this, believe in them and follow them with trust and confidence.

Resourcefulness

For the Christian leader this stems from attitudes of faith in God. They never seem to fear or become overwhelmed by what the future may present them with. They have a built-in competence. They specialise in asking good questions rather than becoming preoccupied with giving good answers.

Faith in people

They trust others despite occasional disappointments. They understand and accept people who are different from them—in ideas as well as personality. They build a team of powerful leaders because they stake their faith in them and do not abandon them when they are down.

Beyond survival

Here are five key steps for leaders as they face the challenge of the future.

Invest in a few people

There is great wisdom in this practice. Democracy is not the key; investing a great deal of your time in a few good people is. Live and think with them.

Invite them to journey with you

Dream with them; build a vision with them.

Weld them into a strong team

Integrate them around difficult, clear-cut goals. Help each of them to find their place of greatest contribution. The way of the empowering leader is selfless. Derive your satisfaction from choosing, coaching and delegating.

Challenge them to master difficult situations

Focus on issues that make them reach for things beyond their grasp.

Demand total integrity at all times

Start with yourself; practise it alone and with your top team.

Permit no one to become involved in duplicity. To succeed, people must face reality and they must face it on a sound moral and spiritual basis.

It might fairly be claimed that these reflect the convictions and practices of the greatest leader of all time—Jesus Christ. Among the parting counsels to his followers, now facing the challenge of their own future as leaders, are these words:

All authority in heaven and on earth has been given to me. Therefore go and make disciples of all nations, baptising them in the name of the Father and of the Son and of the Holy Spirit, and teaching them to obey everything I have commanded you. And surely I am with you always, to the very end of the age (Mt 28:18–20).

They reflect his vision and emphasise his empowerment of them for the task before them. They are recommended to you as you face the challenge of the future.